Save Dr. Jekyll
and
Destroy Mr. Hyde

Stephen White

CREATION HOUSE

SAVE DR. JEKYLL AND DESTROY MR. HYDE by Stephen White
Published by Creation House
A Charisma Media Company
600 Rinehart Road
Lake Mary, Florida 32746
www.charismamedia.com

This book or parts thereof may not be reproduced in any form, stored in a retrieval system, or transmitted in any form by any means—electronic, mechanical, photocopy, recording, or otherwise—without prior written permission of the publisher, except as provided by United States of America copyright law.

Unless otherwise noted, all Scripture quotations are from the King James Version of the Bible.

Scripture quotations marked NKJV are from the New King James Version of the Bible. Copyright © 1979, 1980, 1982 by Thomas Nelson, Inc., publishers. Used by permission.

Scripture quotations marked NLT are from the Holy Bible, New Living Translation, copyright © 1996, 2004, 2007. Used by permission of Tyndale House Publishers, Inc., Wheaton, IL 60189. All rights reserved.

Scripture quotations marked TLB are from The Living Bible. Copyright © 1971. Used by permission of Tyndale House Publishers, Inc., Wheaton, IL 60189. All rights reserved.

Design Director: Bill Johnson
Cover design by Terry Clifton

Copyright © 2014 by Stephen White
All rights reserved.

Library of Congress Cataloging-in-Publication Data: 2013952180
International Standard Book Number: 978-1-62136-697-3
E-book International Standard Book Number: 978-1-62136-698-0

While the author has made every effort to provide accurate telephone numbers and Internet addresses at the time of publication, neither the publisher nor the author assumes any responsibility for errors or for changes that occur after publication.

First edition

14 15 16 17 18 — 987654321
Printed in Canada

DEDICATION

To my family, Daneisha, Nehemiah, Joshua, and Caleb—thanks for your support and prayer. I love you all!

CONTENTS

Chapter One: Curiosity Can Kill....................1

Chapter Two: Contentment 101 9

Chapter Three: Haters Hate; The Chosen Persevere...21

Chapter Four: You Can Run but You Can't Hyde.....35

Chapter Five: Think About What You're Thinking...55

Chapter Six: God's Plan, Our Vision................99

Notes 119

About the Author................................121

Contact the Author 122

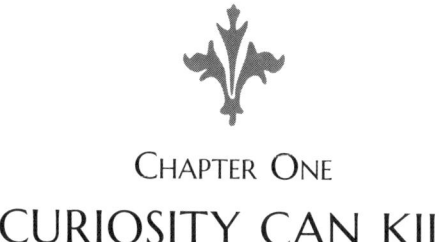

Chapter One
CURIOSITY CAN KILL

In 1886, Robert Louis Stevenson published *Strange Case of Dr. Jekyll and Mr. Hyde*, a tale of a man who made a potion that turned him from a mild-mannered man of science into a vulgar homicidal maniac.

The story reveals the life of an inquisitive scientist who believed with conviction that within each man there are impulses from both a good nature and an evil nature.

To prove his theory, Dr. Jekyll developed a drug to awaken the evil nature within him. The "potion," as he called it, brought out his dark side: the hard-drinking, woman-chasing monster of a man named Mr. Hyde.

Dr. Jekyll confirmed his theory, but to his own detriment. He had become addicted to the potion and the passions of his dark side, which ultimately led to his untimely death.

The truth is we have all found ourselves at some point in the middle of a Dr. Jekyll and Mr. Hyde experience. Drunk with the swagger our darker selves provide, many of us have unintentionally destroyed our dreams, countless opportunities, and any chance at meaningful relationships.

It's frustrating. It's so frustrating that a lot of us loathe who we are or what we have become.

So we start to embrace the monster within, turning to everything and everyone other than God. We start to use remedies that make us sicker, answers that raise more questions, and solutions that cause more problems.[1]

My friends, it is safe to say that our society today is full of bruised and battered *Dr. Jekylls*. They are intelligent, talented, and exceptional people who are slowly but surely falling into an abyss of irrelevance, hopelessness, and mediocrity; maybe not due to purposely giving in to the lusts of their darker selves (although some of us do) but because their evil nature, Mr. Hyde, looks and feels like Godzilla on the rampage.

Instead of standing up to Mr. Hyde, it seems like the good in us is running for cover. So the question is, How did we get ourselves into such a predicament?

Well, I heard a preacher a long time ago tell this story about a bull on a farm that had the perfect life. The pasture was green and long and full of beautiful cows. He was the king of the pasture...the *only* bull on the farm. It was paradise! He had all the food he could eat and all the romance he could stand.

One day two new cows moved into the new farm next door to his. When he saw his new neighbors standing on top of the hill, his heart jumped. He had never seen such beautiful cows in his life.

The only thing that separated the bull and those two beautiful new cows was a tall barbed wire fence.

So every day he stood at the barbed wire fence adoring his new neighbors from afar, fantasizing about meeting them face-to-face one day.

Weeks went by and the bull just couldn't stand it anymore. He had to meet the two most beautiful cows he had ever seen in person. So he backed up a good distance away from the fence, took a deep breath, and then ran toward it as fast as he could.

As he got closer, he gauged the right time to jump and leaped over the barbed wire fence, falling hard to the ground. *Blam!* The barbed wire scratched his underbelly a little, but he didn't care. He was over the fence and could now meet the cows of his dreams!

He ran with excitement and anticipation to the top of the hill where his dream cows were standing…only to find that they were bulls just like him! The moral of the story was he got what he wanted, but lost what he had.

Oftentimes we are so tormented by what we think we want that we lose sight of what God has already given us.

For example, in the Garden of Eden, no one knows why Adam and Eve were hanging out so close to the tree of the knowledge of good and evil. My guess is they were curious. I believe they wanted to see why the tree had such a bad reputation.

The danger of the tree seemed to draw Adam and Eve closer to it. The horror of the tree's capability of taking their lives sparked their curiosity. So they eased their way over to see the deadly tree.

The question is why. They didn't need to know more than what they already knew. They were the king and queen of paradise. Everything was at their fingertips. But maybe that was the problem.

Privilege can often lead to irresponsibility. I believe that was God's reason for setting the rule not to eat of the tree of the knowledge of good and evil in the first place. I believe that God used this rule to try to teach His privileged children to be responsible with how they thought, felt, and behaved.

He wanted them to enjoy the pleasures of what He gave them in the garden, but within reason. But like the bull in our story, they stepped over the boundary of responsibility to try to take advantage of having more than what God had already given them.

Even now at times we can behave like privileged or spoiled children who find themselves in all kinds of trouble just because of something we wanted.

We are so curious about what could be that we oftentimes fail to recognize what God has already made possible.[2]

The truth is the grass is very rarely greener on the other side. How many of you reading this book have had a marriage end, a career destroyed, have burned bridges with friends or loved ones, or have wasted money because you wanted what you saw on someone else's lawn?

Aren't you tired of the same ol' cycle of disappointment, feeling deprived or unhappy, or seeing your life spin out of control? If yes, then it's time for a new strategy.

Are You Satisfied with Your Brand?

In the very beginning of the 1920 cinematic version of Stevenson's published masterpiece, Dr. Jekyll is sitting at a microscope relishing in his recent scientific discovery. He excitedly proclaims to his more conservative friend and colleague, *"I tell you, Lanyon, we haven't begun to discover what science can do with the body and mind of man!"* Dr. Lanyon's reply to his friend's elation was, *"I don't like it! You're tampering with the supernatural!"*[3]

It's evident that God had built Dr. Jekyll to use science as a mechanism to enhance mankind's understanding of the mind and body; because the more we know about ourselves, the better we will live.

It is safe to say that God has built all of humanity to intimately see and understand from various and unique viewpoints the ins and outs of what *He* has created.

In Genesis 1:28, the Lord gives us the responsibility to govern all that He created. He has left it up to us to be innovative enough to take what He has made and increase its viability, strength, and longevity.

So why was Dr. Lanyon, Dr. Jekyll's colleague, so adamantly opposed to what seemed to be a God-given gift? What was it about his friend's discovery that rubbed him the wrong way?

I believe that Dr. Lanyon's response to his friend's findings was to raise a red flag...that Dr. Jekyll's noble pursuit to better mankind through science had taken a peculiar turn.

Like Eve in the garden, I believe that Dr. Jekyll was introduced to an idea that encouraged him to take what God already had in place to be beneficial and turned it into something detrimental. His thirst for knowledge was no longer for the benefit of others (which was the reason he was a gifted scientist in the first place) but to benefit only himself.

Like Eve, the doctor felt deprived in some way and wanted something more. Why? He was an accomplished physician and philanthropist and was well respected.

I have come to the conclusion that Dr. Jekyll did not fully like his true personal "brand."

Our dislike of who we are can oftentimes lead us to do the same: to remake ourselves within a "brand" of a different design.[4]

For example, Satan wasn't always evil. He was a member of the angelic hosts in the kingdom of God, but out of nowhere took a turn for the worse:

> And war broke out in heaven; Michael and his angels fought with the dragon; and the dragon and his angels fought, but they did not prevail.
>
> —REVELATION 12:7–8, NKJV

In Ezekiel 28:15 God expresses from His own lips that Satan, known as Lucifer, the angel of light, before his fall (Isa. 14:12), was perfect in all his ways. God had made him to be the most beautiful and anointed cherub. He was also an accomplished musician; his vocal cords produced sounds of an orchestra:

> The workmanship of thy tabrets and of thy pipes was prepared in thee in the day that thou wast created.
>
> —EZEKIEL 28:13

So what happened? What possessed Satan to think he could overthrow God? Why did he choose to mess up a good thing? Why change his brand when his brand was already one of the hottest commodities on the "universal market"?

I believe that Satan began to think he was something more than what God had made him to be. An idea began to form in his mind:

> I will ascend into heaven, I will exalt my throne above the stars of God: I will sit also upon the mount of the congregation, in the sides of the north: I will ascend above the heights of the clouds; I will be like the most High.
>
> —ISAIAH 14:13–14

He decided that the universe would be better off if he took over! Satan looked at what was on God's lawn and decided it would be better off in his hands!

Isn't that our biggest problem? Why is it so important for us to be the best, to have all eyes on us? Why do we have to be in control of not only our lives but the lives of everyone else? Why do we feel that our will should take precedence over everyone else's, including God's? Does it make our lives better or worse?

Take Satan's life, for instance. His discontent with the greatness he already possessed brought out the worst in him. He ended up giving evil power of attorney over his life and is to this day addicted to demented ambitions.

The beauty and vitality of this being, God's angel of light, had been transformed into the hideous death machine known as the prince of darkness. The good nature in him faded away, and now only the monstrous Hyde remains.

Has he benefited? Only temporarily, because just like Dr. Jekyll, what Satan has custom designed for himself outside of his God-given brand will eventually come to a deadly end.

So the question you have to ask yourself now is, Do you want to fall to the same fate?

CHAPTER TWO
CONTENTMENT 101

One of my favorite horror/monster flicks growing up along with Dr. Jekyll and Mr. Hyde was the 1978 remake of the 1956 film *Invasion of the Body Snatchers*. The movie is about a health inspector who discovers that people are being replaced by replicas grown from plantlike pods. The replicas are clones with the same memories and appearance as the original person, but are emotionless. After the pods duplicate a person while they are sleeping, the original human body is disintegrated. The pod people then would work together to spread more pods so more people could be replaced. Their goal was to take over our world by replacing the entire human race.[1]

In today's world it has become very difficult for an

individual to decipher his/her own perspective of life because it would seem that everybody else has a vested interest in how that individual sees things.

It would seem that we are being forced by family, friends, the media, politicians, etc., to navigate our way through their ideas and opinions and choose which platform to pin our lives on instead of being respected for having any of our own.

One of the reasons why I believe our lives are harder than what they really should be is because we have become replicas of everybody else's opinions and expectations.

And because we are forced to live in such an atmosphere of assimilation, discontent has become a matter of public opinion versus personal assessment.

For example, at the tree of the knowledge of good and evil, the serpent's opinion made Eve feel as though God had deprived her in some way. She began to feel entitled to something better than what she had.

Had Eve personally assessed her own situation, I don't think she would have agreed with what the serpent was selling. She had a good husband, plenty of food to eat, paradise for a home, pets, and no worries. She didn't even have to be concerned with wearing clothes! There were no long hours at the salon, no rushing to the stores for the latest fashions to keep up with public opinion of how she should look, and no going to the gym to keep her shape (there wasn't any fast food or sweets available to make her gain weight, so there was no need for the gym).[2]

So what about you? Have you been buying into what everyone else has been selling about what your life should be like?

Have you become a clone and not a unique individual? Do you care more about fitting in with everyone else, or are you secure in being defined as peculiar?

If you are a Christian, are you looking for a loophole in God's principles of living so that you can continue your pursuit of validation from people who want you to fit in their little box of who they think you are versus who God has predestined you to be?

Do you find yourself looking for an advantage over God's truth about your true brand so that the sting of being different won't feel so bad?

If yes to any of these questions, how do we stop? How do we move ourselves into the realm of contentment with who God has designed us to be? The answer is we have to sever our ties with everyone else's opinion or definition of who we should be, what we should do, or how we should think. Listen to this:

> And do not be conformed to this world, but be transformed by the renewing of your mind, that you may prove what is that good and acceptable and perfect will of God.
> —ROMANS 12:2, NKJV

My friends, God has an interest in painting the universe with the beauty of the real you! He has set things straight through His Son, Jesus Christ, to crucify your darker self and set free the best of who *you* are!

But in order to see your God-given brand come to life, I believe you must choose to strive more adamantly to practice and effectively apply the knowledge and wisdom of the principles of God. By doing so, you will put yourself in position to better understand and recognize the unique brand that specifically expresses your true identity.

During good times and bad times, when the principles of God have free reign in your thinking, in your feelings, and in your ability to choose, I believe life becomes easier to handle and more enjoyable.

So don't continue to live your life as a replica of this world or what other people think. Invest in *your* unique God-given brand.

Contentment Principle #1: Be Content with What You Have and Who You Are

> Let your conversation be without covetousness; and be content with such things as ye have: for he hath said, I will never leave thee, nor forsake thee.
> —Hebrews 13:5

> Moreover whom he did predestinate, them he also called: and whom he called, them he also justified: and whom he justified, them he also glorified. What shall we then say to these things? If God be for us, who can be against us?
> —Romans 8:30–31

What would drive a husband of ten years to cheat on his wife? What would make a person get into thousands of dollars of debt? What convinces some people that they desperately need plastic surgery? A conversation would.

The biggest influence of the many choices we make (or will make in the future) starts with a conversation that involves someone else's viewpoint about one thing or the other.

Some people are good at telling good stories (or lies) about their life experiences to the point that it could influence how we view our own lives. Now life testimonies aren't bad if they possess sustenance such as a lesson learned or a journey to success, etc. But testimonies of indulgence, pleasurable indiscretions, etc., can give the Mr. Hyde in other people ammo to rise and do his dirty work.

Let's be honest. For whatever reason, humanity has a

habit of being easily distracted and intrigued by the forbidden. The more I think about this fact the more I understand why Adam and Eve got into so much trouble: boredom.

What's funny is the boredom many people experience on most occasions isn't even authentic (like Adam and Eve's boredom). Most of the time it's born from a conversation (Eve and the serpent) with someone at the water cooler at work, or a conversation they overheard in the grocery store, or gossip they heard over the phone.

The media plays a big part in our boredom too. Certain commercials, TV shows, and movies can unnecessarily create boredom in the lives of the average Joe. Fantasy becomes more vivid and vital then his own reality and opens the door to complacency, dissatisfaction, and discontent.

It is for this reason that a housewife with a good husband would consider an affair with the gardener, because they heard someone else do it or watched it happen on TV, or a man would have an affair with his best friend's wife because of the conversations he and his best friend had about the couple's sexual exploits.

Or some people who buy stuff because of how other people go on and on about what they or somebody they know just purchased or what they've seen in a magazine or TV commercial. It doesn't even matter whether they can afford it or not. The validation from what other people think of them having these things in their possession is seemingly more important.[3]

Hebrews 13:5 teaches that we can't allow casual conversations to turn into covetousness. Although what we are hearing in a conversation may be tempting to indulge in ourselves, we have to think whether the indulgence is a good choice or fit for us.

Most importantly, I believe we need to get an understanding of what God thinks about what we are talking and thinking about. If a conversation about a certain subject matter could cause damage to what God has predestined in us (Rom. 8:30–31), then we need not involve ourselves in that conversation.

If approached by someone about the fact that you choose not to indulge in gossip or water cooler talk or the "what if I" game of monkey see, monkey do about what someone else saw on TV, at the movies, heard from a friend of a friend, or on DVD, the Internet, and so on, know that you don't have to justify yourself. Be content with the unique brand God has made you to be.

Knowing who God has called you to be affords you to be excited about your own life. It will bring into your life a steady flow of vitality and tranquility; for whom God calls, He justifies; and whom God justifies, He glorifies.

You have nothing to prove to anyone but yourself and God. Always know that God will not make it a point to harshly judge you like other people if you miss "the bar" of your original brand in some way, because His grace is sufficient. He will catch you when you fall and forgive you when you make mistakes. He will lead you back to glory even when you have gone astray.

No longer affected by naysayers, your life becomes the talk of the town. Some may be negative, because haters will hate (we'll talk about that in the next chapter), but others will admire.

Now I'm not condoning that you seek validation from people or expect it, because it doesn't matter. You are now partnering with God to paint the picture of your true brand to the universe. In other words, because *God* validates you by glorifying the brand He has predestined *in* you, others have no choice but to notice.

So if God be for *you*—painting the exquisite portrait of an exceptional individual, loving and appreciating what He sees—then who can be against you?[4]

CONTENTMENT PRINCIPLE #2: FOCUS ON WHAT'S BEST VERSUS FOCUSING ONLY ON WHAT YOU WANT

> Not that I speak in respect of want: for I have learned, in whatsoever state I am, therewith to be content.
>
> —PHILIPPIANS 4:11

Oftentimes our relationship with God and what He has predestined us to be isn't as fulfilling as it could be because of distrust. We don't fully trust God with our lives because various religions have painted an ugly picture of how God sees life.

My friends, our distrust of God can be linked to humanity's misunderstanding of God's true love.

Religion's perspective that God is in complete control over our lives has in many ways diminished the reality of how He prefers to experience them. Let me explain.

In Genesis 2:19 God asked Adam to name all the animals. God didn't really need Adam to name the animals but He *wanted* him to. While Adam named the animals, I believe God got to know His son more intimately. What God had designed on "paper" was now alive in real-time. Every character trait, gift, and ability God built in Adam could now be visible within the natural realm and bring forth its own fruit.

The reality, my friends, is that God wants to see you and me put into action what He has predestined in us. Yes, I believe that God is sovereign and this world is His (Ps. 24). But the fact that He delegated to us authority over what is His (Gen. 1:27–28) and wired us with the ability of free choice, some things—a lot of things—He has left up to us! God's relationship with man is comparable to a father and mother with their newborn babe. Each day their child lives, the more they experience the person the baby truly is. They guide him, they teach him, protect and take care of him, and give him room to grow. They recognize his gifts and invest in them so he can live according to his own destiny.

I believe God prefers to lead us versus control us. He feeds our wisdom and invests in our aspirations to make us stronger, but doesn't force us to use our strengths or abilities to fit His every whim.

God's will for our lives is to be in a partnership with Him. He expects us to come to the table with our passions and ideas to enhance the purpose He has already uniquely assigned us.

Our predestined life has options. We can choose. That's not control. That's love. It's about relationship, not tyranny.

We have become so used to living as *replicas* of a consumer-driven world that we find ourselves disagreeing with God about who we are and what we are capable of becoming. We judge His design for our lives as too rigid or too challenging before we've had the opportunity to truly understand what God sees in us and what He has built us to accomplish.[5]

Humanity's misunderstanding of how much God truly loves them and His desire to invest *in* them has in many ways caused humanity to be insecure and bitter.

Misery loves the confines of its hand-crafted dungeon and despises anyone who tries to release it from its bonds. That's why God has such a hard time getting some of our attention. When God calls upon us to be exceptional, we run away into this dungeon and lock ourselves in, hoping He will leave us alone.

That can't be right, can it? Don't we all want to be great? Don't we all want our lives to mean something and leave a legacy for others to benefit from?

I am sorry to say it is our insecurities about what *can* be through God's plan for us that keeps us on our knees praying for forgiveness for what *shouldn't* have been.

At some point we are going to have to recognize that we can't want more than what we are capable of handling. We can't get caught up in making comparisons between ourselves and other people. Like in our text for this section, we have to learn how to expand our happiness and productivity from whatever state we are currently in.

If you're poor, be faithful with the little that you have. Continue to work toward improving your life, but don't rush. The easy way out is always tempting but very rarely what's best. Our jails are full of poor people who took the easy way out.

Find your God-given niche. No one born on this earth is hapless; we all have a destiny. And I believe if we take the time to get to know God, He will show us how to be rulers over much more than what we have at the moment.

If you're rich, be humble and balance your resources to produce good for you and for your neighbor. What good is it to own everything and not share with people who need help? Why invest in expensive things you probably won't ever use when you can set up some type of foundation or program to give someone else a helping hand?

If you have a good spouse, *don't cheat!* If you have a not-so-good spouse, *don't cheat!* What is lacking in most relationships is honesty. Sharing our feelings honestly and coming to a compromise where both parties function amicably can make a good relationship stronger and a not-so-good relationship better.

Don't let what you want for yourself or for your family hurt you. Teach yourself to recognize what's best to do, say, or apply. Desire is only effective when it is within reason. So focus on what's best and be content that you can't always have everything you want.

Contentment Principle #3: Adapt: Learn How to Take the Bad with the Good

> I know both how to be abased, and I know how to abound: everywhere and in all things I am instructed both to be full and to be hungry, both to abound and to suffer need.
> —Philippians 4:12

Adversity is public enemy number one. It can cause the best of us to fall to our knees and beg for mercy:

> Man that is born of a woman is of few days and full of trouble.
> —Job 14:1

Adversity has no respect of person. If you aren't prepared to deal with adversity and it gets you in its clutches, bad things can happen.

The story of Dr. Jekyll shows us what adversity can cause. You see, Dr. Jekyll was a man of innovation living in a world of intense conservatism. He saw possibilities that no one else cared to give a second thought.

His colleagues' and fellow countrymen's derogatory responses to his work and ideas was what drove him to explore and investigate his darker self. Nice guys finish last, and Dr. Jekyll wanted that to change.

The truth is, no one wants to feel insignificant. Adversity, however, ensures that we do. So our most common response to feeling insignificant is rebellion.

Mr. Hyde is the epitome of rebellion. His "bad boy" persona is often the instrument that many of us use to protect ourselves from feeling irrelevant or disrespected.

But if we learn how to adapt to whatever adversity throws at us then we will be able to manage the negative thoughts or emotions that may come with it.

That's what I love about the apostle Paul and his writings. I believe he was one of the best at dealing with adversity. Here was a man who was beaten, falsely accused, and thrown in jail on a number of occasions, yet was always able to stay true to himself and his God-given brand.

Philippians 4:12 reveals Paul's experience with adversity. He was able to find and experience the best of things during a stage of his life that was at its worst.

My favorite part of this text is, "I am instructed both to be full and to be hungry, both to abound and to suffer need."

Instructed by whom is the question. Like I said in the last section, God wants to see how we can take His original design and expand it. He has provided us with principles in His Word to show us how to be proficient at adapting to any given situation according to our individual strengths and weaknesses. So let's put the principle of Philippians 4:12 into motion.

When life is full of success, handle yourself with care. Make sure you possess a balanced or "down to earth" outlook of where you've been, where you are, and where you are going. Arrogance is an ugly attribute for those who are on top. It's also bait for adversity to take a bite out of your life.

If you hunger, *don't lose your nerve!* The desire to

improve your life or to fulfill aspirations is a good thing; just don't let it drive you to starvation. Research and discover the source of your hunger, because the sustenance you need could already be looking you in the face.

Need validation? Then ask yourself when was the last time you spent quality time with God, yourself, the wife/husband and/or kids.

Need more money? Budget your money and decrease your debt before you try to fix the loophole with three more jobs.

Need more time to create and explore ideas? Then stop working three jobs, budget your money, and decrease your debt!

Need to lose weight? Then eat a balanced diet and exercise according to *your* body type instead of buying every pill or quick fix on the market that continues to enable your bad eating habits.

If life is good, then you should relish in the moment. Thank God for every blessing and enjoy what you have and the relationships that embrace you.

If life is bad, then learn from it. Bad is a state of mind. Tragedy may hurt, but it's not the end of tomorrow. Heartbreak can be devastating, but healing is a gift that God gives to everybody. Mistakes can be depressing, but you can always learn to do better.

If you're in need, there is always hope. There is a Good Samaritan out there waiting to give you a helping hand. God sees your tears and hopes you see His love, compassion, and forgiveness. You're not alone!

Adapt...adapt...adapt![6]

Chapter Three

HATERS HATE; THE CHOSEN PERSEVERE

> And Joseph dreamed a dream, and he told it to his brethren: and they hated him yet the more.
>
> —Genesis 37:5

An opinion is an interpretation, conviction, or assessment developed in the mind about a specific subject, instance, situation, or individual.

In many cases, people hate because of misconceived opinions about various differences between their point of view and someone else's.

Our culture's fascination with being right or superior

and proving that everyone else is wrong or inferior is the cause of our inability to allow hardly anyone to have an opinion or fresh idea.

That being said, someone else's opinion is oftentimes the dagger that kills an individual's dreams.

Some people feel like they need the approval of others in order to gauge their level of success as a productive, likable individual.

I used to be one of them until I realized my God-given brand. I don't have anything to prove to anybody, and neither do you! Our esteem is built on the foundation of who God has predestined us to be versus someone else's opinion or appraisal of who they think we are.

No one else can design what or who we are. There may be people of various influences that God may allow to guide us but never to define us.

Now can we live peaceably, even affectionately, with others whose perspective of our character doesn't necessarily define our true selves? Yes, if we learn how to agree to disagree.

We don't have to agree with someone else's choice of living or their individual impression of our own character. However, just because we disagree with that person's point of view or choice of lifestyle it doesn't give us the right to be hateful, judgmental, spiteful, envious, jealous, or hurtful. Listen to this:

> Judge not, that ye be not judged. For with what judgment ye judge, ye shall be judged: and with what measure ye mete, it shall be measured to you again.
> —MATTHEW 7:1–2

The point I believe Jesus was trying to make in this text is what goes around comes around. What you do or say to others, the same will be done to you.

No wonder so many people's dreams have been lost! Some have spent so much time tearing other people down that they have failed to recognize hatred's destruction of their own destiny!

The reason we chose the story of Joseph to be the center point of this chapter is to show you how to handle yourself when naysayers try to tear you down for having a dream.

Certain people who don't fully understand or agree with your God-given brand may judge you, maybe try to hurt you, stop you, or try to convince others to hurt or stop you.

To protect your esteem, and most importantly your destiny, you have to be adept at dealing with combative people who find offense to your talents, gifts, and perspective of life.

So the next couple of sections in this chapter will focus on showing you how to persevere and navigate through the obstacles people may try to place in front of you.[1]

Principle #1: You Can't Tell Everybody Your Dream

> And Joseph dreamed a dream, and he told it to his brethren: and they hated him yet the more.
> —Genesis 37:5

Telling someone your dreams and aspirations may seem harmless, but in essence telling someone could ruin your opportunity to fulfill them.

Have you ever heard the expression, "You can't tell everybody everything"? Jesus puts it this way:

> Do not let your left hand know what your right hand is doing.
> —MATTHEW 6:3, NKJV

Joseph loved his family and wanted to share his dreams with them. However, Joseph's excitement of seeing *his* destiny with clarity overwhelmed his better judgment and he ended up sharing his dreams with family who didn't like him:

> Now Israel loved Joseph more than all his children, because he was the son of his old age. Also he made him a tunic of many colors. But when his brothers saw that their father loved him more than all his brothers, they hated him and could not speak peaceably to him.
> —GENESIS 37:3–4, NKJV

Sharing his dream with family (who already had something against him) led to a very volatile situation:

> Now when they saw him afar off, even before he came near them, they conspired against him to kill him. Then they said to one another, "Look, this dreamer is coming!... let us now kill him and cast him into some pit....
> "Come and let us sell him to the Ishmaelites, and let not our hand be upon him, for he is our brother and our flesh." ...Then Midianite traders passed by; so the brothers pulled Joseph up and lifted him out of the pit, and sold him to the Ishmaelites for twenty shekels of silver.
> —GENESIS 37:18–20, 27–28, NKJV

Joseph's first lesson on his journey to reach his destiny was humility. His pit experience was the result of his inexperience with how to manage his vision.

The truth is, not everyone can handle what you've been put on this earth to be or accomplish, for a number of reasons:

1. *People have been used to seeing you from their perspective.* Sharing what you believe to be your destiny forces them to redefine their personal appraisal of your capabilities, personality, and frame of mind. Oftentimes this is an uncomfortable and undesirable task for them because now they have to adjust those thoughts that their personal appraisal of you lacked, or did not properly define, or misjudged.

2. *Your dreams and aspirations may reveal their lack of having any.* Jealousy and envy become the fuel to their disdain for you.

3. *Your vision doesn't fit the status quo.* Anything that challenges the frame of mind of the majority, whether it is in business, spirituality, relationships, etc., can be judged as frivolous or lofty thinking.

4. *Your vision puts more control of your life in your hands than in theirs.* This occurs mainly with people who are closest to you.

5. *They may have something against you in some way.* Not every good thing about you will be well liked or accepted. It's sad but true. Some may even have something against you because of the mistakes they have seen you make in your

life, and believe you will make the same mistakes again. They count you out before giving you another chance.

6. *Your destiny doesn't have any room for them.* Some people have a "tag-along" spirit and want what you have and do what you do. If you choose to be something that is too difficult for them to accept or follow, they will try to sabotage your destiny so they won't get left behind.

7. *They just don't like you.* Your connection to them has been based on the principle, "Keep your friends close but your enemies closer!"

To keep your God-given brand from becoming a stumbling block for someone else, you should first consider the pros and cons of "letting the cat out of the bag." Ask yourself:

- Can I trust this person?
- Will they be supportive?
- Can they keep a secret?
- Are they connected to people who could hurt my chances of fulfilling my dreams, or are they connected to people who could become valuable resources to my dream?

Also be aware that your dreams and aspirations could cause adversity in certain situations. Honestly speaking, people don't see what you see, so you have to expect conflict of some kind.

So be careful of how you express your goals. Some people will be able to handle your transformation and some won't. You will have to learn how to read people in various situations—especially with those who know you best.

Don't let your left hand know what your right hand is doing. Your destiny is a secret between you and God. Be patient in choosing the right people to partner with to accomplish your dreams.

At the proper moment, the fruit your destiny bears will reveal itself at the right moment for everyone else to see!

Principle #2: When All Is Well...Look for the Appearance of a Saboteur

> The Lord was with Joseph, and he was a successful man; and he was in the house of his master the Egyptian. And his master saw that the Lord was with him and that the Lord made all he did to prosper in his hand...So it was, from that time that he had made him overseer of his house and all that he had, that the Lord blessed the Egyptian's house for Joseph's sake....
>
> And it came to pass after these things that the master's wife cast longing eyes on Joseph, and she said, "Lie with me." But he refused....
>
> She caught him by his garment, saying, "Lie with me." But he left his garment in her hand and fled...when she saw that he had left his garment in her hand and fled outside, that she called to the men of her house and spoke to them, saying, "See, he has brought in to us a Hebrew to mock us. He came in to me to lie with me, and I cried out with a loud voice. And it happened, when he heard that I lifted my voice and cried out, that he left his garment with me, and fled and went outside....
>
> So it was, when his master heard the words

which his wife spoke to him...that his anger was aroused. Then Joseph's master took him and put him into the prison.

—GENESIS 39:2–5, 7–8, 11–15, 19–20, NKJV

Joseph found a way to be successful even though he was in a less than favorable situation. His brothers had sold him into slavery, but Joseph didn't let his plight keep him from working hard or doing the right thing.

Joseph's valiant efforts had earned him the respect of his boss, Potiphar, and he was given a promotion as the overseer or manager of his boss's whole house. Every servant, maid, farm hand, etc., that was employed by the Egyptian was now under Joseph's charge. All was going well.

But drama hit. His boss's wife desired to have an affair with him. Joseph still kept a level head and didn't allow his darker self to convince him to take advantage of a sinful opportunity. But the woman was determined and persistent. One day she saw an opening to grab Joseph and entice him to have an affair.

Being the good man that Joseph was, he refused and fled. His dream was still in the forefront of his thinking, and having an affair with his boss's wife would have ruined his chances to reach his destiny.

Feeling rejected, Potiphar's wife framed Joseph with accusations that he tried to rape her, and Joseph was thrown into prison.

Joseph's story proves that adversity couldn't care less about anyone doing the right thing on a consistent basis. It will show up on your best of days and hit you with everything in its arsenal to try to stop you in your tracks.

But with God in your life, adversity is immediately demoted from absolute chaos to a profitable learning experience.

Instead of dealing with a mountain of stress, trouble,

injustice, and an army of enemies, by His grace your toughest storms are shrunk into little waves of stepping stones in character, training sessions on how to adapt, recon and defeat of enemies, and the recognition of the pros and cons of how you handle trouble or your inadequacies:[2]

> And we know that all things work together for good to those who love God, to those who are the called according to His purpose.
> —ROMANS 8:28, NKJV

The actions of Potiphar's wife are a typical example of what people are capable of when they can't get what they want out of people or when they see others on the rise while their lives stand still.

Like crabs in a barrel, when one has found the courage to escape the confines of mediocrity the others latch on to stop them.

Many people latch on to others who are doing well because of their own lack of initiative. They may not purposely mean you harm but can cause harm nonetheless.

However, the true saboteur is heartless and without remorse. They can't stand your success or progression. So they set out to manipulate you under their control or set you up for a fall.

Rumors, gossip, blackmail, betrayal, spite, and false accusations are their weapons of choice. Potiphar's wife chose spite and false accusation. She may have thought to herself, "Who is this Hebrew slave refusing the beauty of an Egyptian woman?"

Her spiteful malice toward Joseph's rejection of her advances led her to falsely accuse Joseph of something he didn't do.

But as you will see in the next section, your God-given

brand carries the favor of God. So no matter what kind of saboteur has you in their sights, every negative thing they plot against you God will use to bless you; because all things work together for *your* good!

Principle #3: Failures Are the Launching Pads for Success

> Potiphar was furious when he heard his wife's story about how Joseph had treated her. So he took Joseph and threw him into the prison where the king's prisoners were held, and there he remained.
> But the LORD was with Joseph in the prison and showed him his faithful love. And the LORD made Joseph a favorite with the prison warden. Before long, the warden put Joseph in charge of all the other prisoners and over everything that happened in the prison. The warden had no more worries, because Joseph took care of everything. The LORD was with him and caused everything he did to succeed.
> —Genesis 39:19–23, NLT

When you're walking in the lane of your God-given destiny, all things are possible! Even in the darkest of moments, triumph is the order of the day!

Perfectly designing events to try to crumble this young man's life, adversity thought it had put a halt to Joseph's ambition for greatness.

You see, adversity wanted Joseph to feel like a nobody—like a failure—so he would quit and miss out on his destiny.

But the love of God Joseph experienced on the inside drove him to carry on.

He was thrown into a pit by those who were closest to

him but never lost hope. He was sold into slavery but made the best of a situation that could have been the death of his self-esteem. He was unfairly accused and thrown into jail but still prevailed as a man of valor and value. Joseph had God's favor.

Favor isn't something you earn, but what God gives freely.

I believe that Joseph received God's favor because he truly believed his dream of being great. He believed that God had made him to be someone special. So when adversity took shots at him, he turned the other cheek! He paid adversity no attention! The vision of his destiny was too real to him to think that anything could stop him. He thought that if God believed in him, then what did he have to lose?[3]

Failure did not confine him. It only made him better. He was stronger, bolder, and more determined than ever before:

> Pharaoh's chief cup-bearer and chief baker offended their royal master. Pharaoh became angry with these two officials, and he put them in the prison where Joseph was... and the captain of the guard assigned them to Joseph, who looked after them. While they were in prison, Pharaoh's cup-bearer and baker each had a dream one night, and each dream had its own meaning. When Joseph saw them the next morning, he noticed that they both looked upset. "Why do you look so worried today?" he asked them. And they replied, "We both had dreams last night, but no one can tell us what they mean."
>
> "Interpreting dreams is God's business," Joseph replied. "Go ahead and tell me your dreams."
>
> —GENESIS 40:1–8, NLT

Joseph understood what the two men were going through. He knew what it felt like to be misunderstood and cast down. So he took the opportunity to show these two men the same love God had shown him and helped them to understand their dreams and destiny.

Jesus Christ, the Son of God, was also misunderstood and cast down. He had a dream: to save men from the Hyde that ailed them and to endow the Jekyll God designed them to be.

He died a death that looked to be His biggest failure, but became His most celebrated triumph! He had succeeded; He rose from death's grip so that all men could launch the best of themselves from the platform of every failure the worst of them provided. His compassion opened the door for all men to fulfill their God-given purpose.[4]

It was Joseph's gesture of compassion for the baker and the king's cupbearer that opened the door to his own destiny:

> So [Pharaoh] called for all the magicians and wise men of Egypt. When Pharaoh told them his dreams, not one of them could tell him what they meant.
>
> Finally, the king's chief cup-bearer spoke up. "Today I have been reminded of my failure," he told Pharaoh. "Some time ago, you were angry with the chief baker and me, and you imprisoned us in the palace of the captain of the guard. One night the chief baker and I each had a dream, and each dream had its own meaning. There was a young Hebrew man with us in the prison who was a slave of the captain of the guard. We told him our dreams, and he told us what each of our dreams meant. And everything happened just as he had predicted. I was restored to my position as

cup-bearer, and the chief baker was executed and impaled on a pole."

Pharaoh sent for Joseph at once, and he was quickly brought from the prison. After he shaved and changed his clothes, he went in and stood before Pharaoh. Then Pharaoh said to Joseph, "I had a dream last night, and no one here can tell me what it means. But I have heard that when you hear about a dream you can interpret it."...

Joseph's suggestions were well received by Pharaoh and his officials. So Pharaoh asked his officials, "Can we find anyone else like this man so obviously filled with the spirit of God?" Then Pharaoh said to Joseph, "Since God has revealed the meaning of the dreams to you, clearly no one else is as intelligent or wise as you are. You will be in charge of my court, and all my people will take orders from you. Only I, sitting on my throne, will have a rank higher than yours."

Pharaoh said to Joseph, "I hereby put you in charge of the entire land of Egypt." Then Pharaoh removed his signet ring from his hand and placed it on Joseph's finger. He dressed him in fine linen clothing and hung a gold chain around his neck. Then he had Joseph ride in the chariot reserved for his second-in-command. And wherever Joseph went, the command was shouted, "Kneel down!" So Pharaoh put Joseph in charge of all Egypt. And Pharaoh said to him, "I am Pharaoh, but no one will lift a hand or foot in the entire land of Egypt without your approval."

—GENESIS 41:8–15, 37–44, NLT

No one is lost; even when stuck in the dungeons of disenfranchisement, victory is right around the corner if you continue to believe!

So count every failure as a launching post. Examine it and learn from it. See the pros and cons and set new standards for yourself. Engage in a conversation with God to better understand how to operate effectively, efficiently, and proficiently within your brand.

You can make it! You can live your dream! You can enjoy life! You can love and respect yourself! Nothing can stop you! You are the gift of God that was built to keep on giving!

Chapter Four

YOU CAN RUN BUT YOU CAN'T HYDE

> I find then a law, that, when I would do good, evil is present with me.
> —Romans 7:21

Evil is a phenomenon whose definition has been lost in translation. Evil to one person could be interpreted as something good by another. The chaos of our world signifies such a fact.

So what is evil's true face? How can we identify with conviction wrong versus right?

First we must identify our origin. Were we built to be both good *and* evil, or just good? Let's check and see:

> So God created man in his own image, in the image of God created he him; male and female created he them. And God blessed them, and God said unto them, Be fruitful and multiply, and replenish the earth, and subdue it: and have dominion over the fish of the sea, and over the fowl of the air, and over every living thing that moveth upon the earth....And God saw every thing that he had made, and behold, it was very good.
> —GENESIS 1:27–28, 31

Based on the text above, evil was excluded from man's makeup. God uses words like blessed (favor), fruitful (productive), multiply (expand), replenish (not wasteful, restore), subdue (manage), and dominion (leadership) to describe man's nature.

Man was born as God's child...a natural image of supernatural likeness:

> And the LORD God formed man out of the dust of the ground, and breathed into his nostrils the breath of life; and man became a living soul.
> —GENESIS 2:7

> God is light, and in him is no darkness at all....God is love; and he that dwelleth in love dwelleth in God, and God in him.
> —1 JOHN 1:5; 4:16

The question arises then, Where did evil come from? How did it get a hold of us? And when we want to do good, why is evil always present?

Well, my friends, I have learned that just as God *is* good, evil has the possibility *to be*.

I'm definitely not saying that God *Himself* is evil,

because we know that there is no evil or darkness in Him (1 John 1:5), but God has always created life with the freedom of choice.

Therefore, there is always a chance that someone could decide to go in the opposite direction away from God. In other words, every life, supernatural or natural, that was or is born had or has the opportunity to veto God.

Those of us who veto God, however, can become susceptible to evil characteristics. Let me give you some examples:

- God's love for us inspires us to love others. Evil's love of using and abusing us makes us comfortable with using and abusing others.

- God protects us, so we try to protect others. Evil hurts us, so we end up hurting others.

- God teaches us to be good; therefore, we bless others and are blessed ourselves. Evil teaches us to do wrong; therefore, we curse others and ourselves.

- God supplies principles to ensure a viable and prosperous future. Evil supplies sinful vices to enslave us and minimize our greatness to ensure its own future.

- God is a spirit that loves us for who we are. Evil is a beast of burden that always makes us feel we aren't good enough.

- God supplies our need; therefore, we desire to help others meet their needs. Evil harvests us to fulfill its own desires; therefore, we use others to supply our own selfish ambition.

Let's face facts. Evil has always been the vampire of our universe. All it takes to awaken him from his coffin is a veto of what God has predestined in our lives. Even those of us who claim our works in His name better be careful that our works actually match His goodness. Because those who use His name to do evil or hurt others will be held accountable:

> Many will say to me in that day, Lord, Lord, have we not prophesied in thy name? and in thy name have cast out devils? and in thy name done many wonderful works? And then will I profess unto them, I never knew you: depart from me, ye that work iniquity.
> —MATTHEW 7:22–23

Lucifer's transformation from the angel of light to Satan, the prince of darkness, is a perfect example of evil being awakened via veto of a God-given brand.

I know what you're thinking. You may be wondering why it's wrong to veto God and build your own destiny, especially if God has given us the right to make that choice.

Well, based on religion's lust to condemn, it would seem that God regrets giving us the freedom to choose. This idea has caused many people to believe that God is unfair, so they rebel against Him.

According to religion, all who choose to build their own destiny God hates and will punish. But that's not the real picture:

> I am the good shepherd, and know my sheep, and am known of mine. As the Father knoweth me, even so I know the Father: and I lay down my life for the sheep. And other sheep I have, which are

> not of this fold: them also I must bring, and they shall hear my voice; and there shall be one fold.
> —John 10:14–16

> The Lord is not slack concerning his promise, as some men count slackness; but is longsuffering to us-ward, not willing that any should perish, but that all should come to repentance.
> —2 Peter 3:9

"Repentance?" you ask. "Why repent of what You gave me the right to do?" you proclaim. These questions and others like them are what we will give answers to and principles for in the next few chapters.

The more we educate ourselves on what evil truly is, the more loving and caring we will see God has always been.[1]

The Birds and the Bees about Evil

> And the Lord God commanded the man, saying, Of every tree of the garden thou mayest freely eat: But of the tree of the knowledge of good and evil, thou shalt not eat of it: for in the day thou eatest thereof thou shalt surely die.
> —Genesis 2:16–17

The question that often arises is, "If God wanted man to be good, why would He put the tree of the knowledge of good *and* evil in the garden?"

It's simple. God learns from experience. The more intimate the relationship He has with an individual, the more likely He will encounter what He has predestined *within* that individual.

Remember, we are made to make our own choices. By *His* sovereign choice and authority, God looks to savor what He creates, not enslave it.

And because our relationship with Him is founded on love, He chooses to allow us to be ourselves without interference. He may question why we think the way we do or behave the way we do, but *never* takes it upon Himself to force you or me to change how we choose to think or what we decide to do. Like a loving parent who cares:

1. *He warns.* He can see what we can't see, so He gives us heads up or sets up guiding posts before we stumble into something that would hurt our chances of being great or enjoying life to the fullest.

2. *He chastises who He loves.* He will allow the consequences of our bad decisions, habits, or mistakes to "spank us" or cause a "time-out" moment in our lives in hope that we will see the error of our ways.

3. *He forgives.* He is more than happy to give us another chance if we are responsible enough to confess our wrongdoing and ask to be forgiven.

4. *He rebuilds.* He will reveal how you can fix what you broke or what someone else destroyed.

5. *He restores.* His faith in you and willingness to give you another chance replenishes your faith in yourself and your trust in Him. Guilt and condemnation become a thing of the past.

6. *He revives.* What we murder in our character that was built to sustain our sanity, self-respect, and ability to love, God desires to resurrect and upgrade.

7. *He teaches.* God is the Dean of the universe. Every subject that is a necessity to the

implementation of your God-given brand He will teach, discuss, and make plain. He guides us to our destiny through failures, trials, tribulations, obstacles, distresses, or persecutions.[2]

With this in mind, let's answer the question, "If God wanted man to be good, why would He put the tree of the knowledge of good *and* evil in the garden?"

First, let's pinpoint what God learned from His experience with Lucifer. Isaiah 14:13–14 reveals Lucifer's revelation to design his own brand:

> "I will ascend into heaven, I will exalt my throne above the stars of God: I will sit also upon the mount of the congregation, in the sides of the north: I will ascend above the heights of the clouds; I will be like the most High."

God learned from His experience with Lucifer that the privileges He endows His creatures with need to have buffers; not buffers to enslave, but to guide and improve.

Lucifer made a choice. Was God happy about it? I think not. Would you be happy if you saw your son convince a third of your kingdom to rebel against you?

But God is longsuffering. When we rebel or make mistakes He wants to know why. His decision on how to deal with our actions will be based on our reason(s) for transgressing against Him.

God didn't make a move on Lucifer's rebellion until Lucifer got too big for his britches:

> And war broke out in heaven: Michael and his angels fought with the dragon; and the dragon and his angels fought, but they did not prevail....
> Then I saw an angel coming down from heaven,

> having the key to the bottomless pit and a great chain in his hand. He laid hold of the dragon, that serpent of old, who is the Devil and Satan, and bound him for a thousand years...that he should deceive the nations no more till the thousand years were finished...
> —REVELATION 12:7–8; 20:1–3, NKJV

Did Lucifer—now known as Satan, the devil, or as our text states, "the dragon"—repent of his mistake? No.

Does God still love him? Yes. God hates the evil in us, but loves each individual that He has created, for all were created for His pleasure (Rev. 4:11), which includes Lucifer and his new self-made identity.

Why else would God allow him to grace heaven every now and again (Job 1:6–7) and use Lucifer's new identity as a buffer to the rest of us (Job 1:8, 2 Cor. 12:7)? Confused? Maybe you're doubtful? Let's dig a little deeper.

As we stated earlier, God learned that the privileges He endows His creatures with need to have buffers; not buffers to enslave, but to guide and improve.

So when God created Adam and set him in the middle of paradise, He strategically placed a buffer in the garden to keep Adam grounded:

> And the LORD God commanded the man, saying, Of every tree of the garden thou mayest freely eat: But of the tree of the knowledge of good and evil, thou shalt not eat of it: for in the day that thou eatest thereof thou shalt surely die.
> —GENESIS 2:16–17

At the same time, God released His prodigal son, Satan (Rev. 20:7–8), in hope that the event would fortify and bring to life Adam and Eve's God-given brand (Gen.

1:28–30) on how to deal with adversity and their ability to manage the privileges afforded to them. God used this same strategy with Job (Job 1:8).

In Genesis 3:1 (NKJV), we see the devil challenge Eve's understanding of God's principle and her ability to apply it. What's interesting is he doesn't challenge her understanding of the tree of the knowledge of good and evil itself. He simply places doubt in her head about what God said about the tree by twisting words. He asks Eve, *"Has God indeed said, 'You shall not eat of every tree of the garden'?"*

God never said that *every* tree was off limits…just one.

The serpent, as Satan is also called, challenged Eve to prove her faith in what God said. Listen to her response:

> "We may eat the fruit of the trees of the garden; but of the tree which is in the midst of the garden, God has said, 'You shall not eat it, nor shall you touch it, lest you die.'"
> —Genesis 3:3, NKJV

Eve embellishes on God's principle a bit by adding that death would not only come if you ate of the tree of the knowledge of good and evil, but also if you touched it.

Here lies many Christians' downfall. People embellish on God's principles because they have doubts. They may lash out in judgment of others because they may not fully believe in God's principles themselves. So to hide the notion of a lack of faith, they cover it with condemnation or make up their own God-like principles that are built on half-truths.

Seeing that Eve was unsure of the meaning of God's principle, Satan takes a potshot at God's Word:

> And the serpent said unto the woman, Ye shall not surely die: For God doth know that in the day ye eat thereof, then your eyes shall be opened, and ye shall be as gods, knowing good and evil.
> —Genesis 3:4–5

Satan's opinion influenced Eve to doubt God. She began to question God's intentions and His trustworthiness. So what did her doubt produce? Let's take a peek:

> The woman saw that the tree was good for food, that it was pleasant to the eyes, and a tree desirable to make one wise.
> —Genesis 3:6a, nkjv

Eve began to want what she thought the fruit had to offer. Her desire stirred her senses:

- Her eyes attested to the fruit's beauty.
- Her nose inhaled the aroma of something good to eat.
- Her taste buds became wet and her stomach growled in hunger.

With her senses now on red alert, she begins to feel deprived:

- "God didn't tell us everything…what does He have to hide?"
- "How could God be so stingy…I thought He loved us."
- "The serpent told the truth…he's my friend."

- "I'm going to eat this fruit and dare God to kill me…I'll be just like Him anyway, so what does it matter?"

Now what is mind boggling about all this is that Adam is with Eve the whole time during her conversation with the devil.

God gave Adam the principle of not eating of the tree of the knowledge of good and evil first. It was his job to teach Eve God's principle. So what happened? "Yes dear," is what happened:

> She took of its fruit and ate. She also gave to her husband with her, and he ate.
> —Genesis 3:6b, nkjv

The beauty of Eve—her smell, her touch, the softness of her skin, her curvy figure, the sound of her soft voice—drove Adam temporarily insane!

Adam knew the consequence of eating from the tree of the knowledge of good and evil but couldn't think of the right thing to do at the time worth two cents! All he saw was how good Eve looked holding the forbidden fruit in her hand!

You would think that the notion of "death" would have stirred up some common sense within Adam. But that's what happens when Hyde takes over. Nothing makes sense.

Adam found himself in the same predicament as Eve. As Eve took a bite out of the forbidden fruit, his senses began to stir:

- His eyes began to see his wife's beauty in a more seductive light.

- Watching her dangerous demeanor made him lust for her.
- His body burned to feel her touch.

With his senses now on red alert, he decides to set aside good sense to do the right thing in order to please his wife, hoping that later on she would allow him to enjoy the pleasures of his lustful fantasies of her.

So here it is, my brothers and sisters. The birds and the bees of evil:

> Let no man say when he is tempted, I am tempted of God: for God cannot be tempted with evil, neither tempteth he any man: But every man is tempted, when he is drawn away of his own lust, and enticed.
> —JAMES 1:13–14

Now there is a huge difference between *tempt* and *test*. Releasing Satan and allowing him to confront Adam and Eve was a test. After God's experience with His son Lucifer's choice to give in to evil, God decided to evaluate Adam and Eve's knowledge of what He had taught them.

It was a test of distinction: to distinguish between what's right (God's principle) vs. what's wrong (Satan's apostasy). God wanted to educate His children of the possibilities of evil impulses and ideas and their consequences, and that Adam and Eve's choices would shape their lives for the better or for the worse. It's a strategy He still uses to this day (1 Pet. 1:7).

To tempt someone, however, is to take advantage of someone else's weaknesses for your own accord. That's why God doesn't tempt man; He tests man. He looks to bring out the best in us, not the worst.

The serpent tempted Adam and Eve, but indirectly. He merely gave his opinion and suggested that if *they* chose to eat the fruit everything would be OK.

Now did he have an ulterior motive? Sure he did. He saw Adam and Eve as a means to an end, a way of escape or an opportunity to finish what he had started in heaven.

But the situation was never in the serpent's hands. It never is. The tempter has no power. The power is always in the hands of the one being tempted (James 1:12). It's up to the one being tempted to choose whether to give in or not.

It was Adam and Eve who possessed the right to either listen and accept Satan's suggestion or ignore and reject Satan's suggestion (which is what I believe to be the main focus of God's test).

What convinced Adam and Eve to rebel against the principle that God created to help keep them grounded was their own lust to act on what they heard.

When Adam and Eve made the choice to veto God's principle, a traumatic event occurred:

> Then the eyes of both of them were opened, and they knew that they were naked; and they sewed fig leaves together and made themselves coverings.
> —Genesis 3:7, NKJV

Their eyes had been opened to a world of humiliation. Guilt and shame had revealed inadequacies that Adam and Eve weren't ready to mentally or emotionally handle:

> And they heard the sound of the Lord God walking in the garden in the cool of the day, and Adam and his wife hid themselves from the presence of the Lord God among the trees of the garden. Then the Lord God called to Adam and said to him, "Where are you?" So [Adam] said, "I

> heard your voice in the garden, and I was afraid because I was naked; and I hid myself."
> —GENESIS 3:8–10, NKJV

Anxiety set in. Adam and Eve became fearful of what God was going to do to them. They were now well aware of their mistake and knew that punishment was coming.

Now I want you to pay close attention to God's reaction:

> And [God] said, "Who told you that you were naked? Have you eaten from the tree of which I commanded that you should not eat?"
> —GENESIS 3:11, NKJV

Now the moment Adam and Eve bit into the forbidden fruit, God could have struck them down immediately. That was the rule, right? So the question remains, why didn't He?

It was a test. Instead of punishing them straightaway, God decided to use this moment of indiscretion as a tool to educate His children.

I believe God gave them an opportunity to get an understanding of why their choice was a mistake so that He could provide them with a number of possible strategies on how to avoid a similar situation.

I believe that God also took the opportunity to give Adam and Eve the chance to ask Him questions, voice their concerns, and explain their reasons for what just happened; in other words, God opened up a dialogue to give His children an opportunity to redeem themselves.

This is why repentance is so vitally important; it's the foundation for redemption.

OK, now pay close attention to Adam's response to God's question:

> Then the man said, "The woman who you gave to be with me, she gave me of the tree, and I ate."
>
> —Genesis 3:12, nkjv

Uh oh! That was the wrong answer! Anger sets in against God. Adam blames God for the woman He gave him and then blames the woman for *his* actions.

How could Adam do such a thing? It was God who recognized (even before it happened) Adam's demeanor as he named the animals (Gen. 2:19–20) and felt that it wasn't good for Adam to be alone, and created Eve to fulfill what Adam had desire for in his heart (Gen. 2:21–23; Rom. 8:29).

Also, how could Adam get angry with God when it was Adam's responsibility to look after Eve in the first place? God presented the rule to Adam first, so why didn't he choose to act on what *he* knew was right?

I believe the answer is Adam's lust for Eve's "bad girl" antics. We could also conclude that the serpent's perspective caught Adam's attention as well.

Adam ate the fruit because *he* chose to, not because his wife forced him (James 1:13–14).

After hearing Adam play the blame game and not take responsibility for his actions, God continues His investigation and turns to Eve:

> And the Lord God said to the woman "What is this you have done?"
>
> —Genesis 3:13a, nkjv

Eve follows suit and responds to God in a similar manner as Adam, but with coy:

> "The serpent [devil] deceived me, and I ate."
>
> —Genesis 3:13b, nkjv

In essence, Eve's response was, "The devil made me do it!" It was another faulty answer that ran away from personal responsibility.

Now pay close attention, my friends. God *did not* make judgment on Adam and Eve until after He *heard* their explanations! As a matter of fact, God stood up for His children:

> And the LORD God said unto the serpent, Because thou hast done this, thou art cursed above all cattle, and above every beast of the field; upon thy belly shalt thou go, and dust shalt thou eat all the days of thy life:
> And I will put enmity between thee and the woman, and between thy seed and her seed; it shall bruise thy head, and thou shalt bruise his heel.
> —GENESIS 3:14–15

Basically, God tells His prodigal son Satan that nothing has changed; man will still be heirs to His kingdom and rulers of the earth. He also made clear to His prodigal son that his final judgment for his iniquities was inevitable (Rev. 20:10) and would be handed to him through the lineage of man.

Genesis 3:15 is the prophecy of Christ being born of a woman and the promise of the realignment of all that Satan had a hand in destroying.

It is at this point that God sets the path for Jesus to restore man mentally, emotionally, soulically, spiritually, and eternally.

At the same time, His children had to be punished. Their irresponsible actions and unremorseful responses led God to keep His promise of punishing them. If we fail in the same manner as Adam and Eve, then we will share the same fate.

But don't be discouraged. Death, my friends, is not the end of things, but the beginning of something else. It is transition from one position to the next physically, spiritually, and eternally.

In this particular case, death was the temporary separation from God and the eternal inheritance thereof:

> Therefore the Lord God sent him forth from the garden of Eden, to till the ground from whence he was taken. So he drove out the man; and he placed at the east of the garden of Eden Cherubims, and a flaming sword which turned every way, to keep the way of the tree of life.
> —Genesis 3:23–24

Man's immortality was taken from him:

> "For you were made from dust, and to dust you will return."
> —Genesis 3:19, nlt

> For the wages of sin is death.
> —Romans 6:23

Adam and Eve were punished individually. However, their individual punishments would be passed down from generation to generation until the day of redemption through Jesus Christ:

> For as by one man's disobedience many were made sinners, so by the obedience of one shall many be made righteous.
> —Romans 5:19

Man now had to fight Satan for what was rightfully his:

> For we are not fighting against flesh-and-blood enemies, but against evil rulers and authorities of the unseen world, against mighty powers in this dark world, and against evil spirits in the heavenly places.
>
> —Ephesians 6:12, NLT

Adam and Eve's bad choice to seek after a brand outside of the one God had already given them transferred authority over to Satan and gave him access to an inheritance that wasn't meant for him.

Always remember, my friends, that Satan can't create. He can only suggest, intimidate, and beguile. He has to steal our inheritance by fooling us into signing a power of attorney through sinful behavior.

He will then take that power of attorney and force us into slavery. As slaves, Satan uses our gifts and talents to build his kingdom.

Are you still wondering why repentance is important? Repentance can save you from the awful fate of sin:

> If you confess with your mouth the Lord Jesus and believe in your heart that God raised Him from the dead, you will be saved. For with the heart one believes unto righteousness, and with the mouth confession is made unto salvation. For the Scripture says, "Whoever believes on Him will not be put to shame." For there is no distinction between Jew and Greek [Gentile], for the same Lord over all is rich to all who call upon Him. For "whoever calls on the name of the Lord shall be saved."
>
> —Romans 10:9–13, NKJV

"What?" you scream in offense. "God was the one who took the risk!" you insist.

You're right. God was the one who took the risk. He took the risk because He loved them. That's what love is; taking the risk of giving yourself to and believing in someone unconditionally, and hoping that someone will love you in the same manner.

So don't blame God for taking the risk to trust and have faith in whom He loves. Instead, learn from Adam and Eve's goof up and think about taking the opportunity to get to know God and the love He is willing to give.

Now don't get down on Adam and Eve. They were rookies and had to learn from their experience.

It's the same with us. The reason our lives may be off course is because we are inexperienced in managing and applying our God-given brand.

So just because evil is present doesn't mean we have to listen or take its suggestions to heart. We decide. It's our life and our responsibility.

God has set the playing field and the rules of the game. Whether we win or lose will be determined by how well *we* choose to play.[3]

Chapter Five
THINK ABOUT WHAT YOU'RE THINKING

> Guard your heart above all else, for it determines the course of your life.
> —Proverbs 4:23, NLT

THE HEART OF human function is the mind. It is the driving force that governs the trademark of an individual's life and the animation thereof.

The mind is made up of three faculties: thought, emotion, and the will. The most important of these three, in my opinion, is the faculty of thought.

Thoughts are the building blocks of principles that evaluate and commission a perspective of life wherein our feelings find validity and our choices receive direction. Therefore, if our thoughts are out of whack then we will most likely create a path of life that is out of whack.

Take Dr. Jekyll, for example. His unfortunate fate came from his inability to manage the thoughts that arose from antagonistic opinions that challenged the soundness of how he thought and felt about himself and the course of life he had chosen:[1]

> Sir George turns and looks at Dr. Jekyll with malcontent...pauses...and says, "In devoting yourself to others Dr. Jekyll, aren't you neglecting the development of yourself?"
>
> Dr. Jekyll answers Sir George's question with compassion, "Isn't it by serving others that one develops oneself?"

At first glance, the philanthropic principles by which Dr. Jekyll lived disputed Sir George's opposing opinions of his character.

But Sir George's bombardment of Dr. Jekyll's true self hit a weak spot:

> Disgusted at Dr. Jekyll's reply, Sir George responds, "Which self? A man has two; as he has two hands. Just because I'm right handed doesn't mean I shouldn't use my left." Sir George goes on and maliciously states, "I believe that a really strong man fears nothing. It is the weak man that fears experience."
>
> Dr. Jekyll shifts uncomfortably in his chair clinching his glass of wine as he listens with a look of confusion and torment on his face.

Instead of holding true to who Dr. Jekyll knew he was, he allowed Sir George's opinion to cause damage to his mind.

The damage is twofold. First, Sir George's dogmatic demeanor caused Dr. Jekyll to feel inferior. Dr. Jekyll was used to being the authority over how he thought, but being confronted by a seemingly superior opponent diminished that authority, causing Dr. Jekyll to let his guard down and contemplate the concept that Sir George introduced.

Secondly, Dr. Jekyll felt insecure about his self-worth and the direction of his life because of Sir George's casual judgment that Dr. Jekyll's "goody two-shoes" lifestyle made him weak.

All that was needed now for Sir George to "reform" Dr. Jekyll's philanthropic personality was an instrument of enticement:

> Sir George sees that Dr. Jekyll is wrestling with his thoughts and deliberately continues to assault Dr. Jekyll's good nature, "A man cannot destroy the savage in him by denying its impulses. The only way to get rid of temptation is to yield to it!"
>
> Dr. Jekyll's body language reveals that he is perplexed but curious.
>
> Sir George realizes that he has Dr. Jekyll right where he wants him and convinces Dr. Jekyll to come along with him and the other noblemen to a gentlemen's club.
>
> They enter the club and sit in a secluded area in the back. As they're sitting, Dr. Jekyll is petrified of what he sees before him. There in front of the club on a small stage, beautiful and provocatively dressed women dance seductively.
>
> One dancer in particular catches his eye.

The provocative dancers served as the instrument to tempt Dr. Jekyll to rethink a different course from his already successful, good-natured life.

The only reason Dr. Jekyll didn't immediately give in to what he heard and what he saw was because his philanthropic personality (the foundation of Dr. Jekyll's God-given brand) was putting up a fight.

However, Dr. Jekyll's fight was difficult because his natural instincts as a heterosexual male were being enticed to experience a woman who seductively offered those same instincts a door of opportunity:

> As the dancer comes toward them, Sir George reaches for her but she surpasses him and heads straight for Dr. Jekyll.
>
> She vivaciously rubs her hands on Dr. Jekyll's chest and shoulders and asks, "Would you like for me to dance for you?" Dr. Jekyll says nothing. He grabs her arms as she continues to gently caress him and lustfully stares into her eyes, then at her hands, then her skin, and then her voluptuous figure.

Even during this moment of temptation Dr. Jekyll's principles of thought put up a fight:

> Noticing that he was not himself and perhaps remembering that he was involved with Millicent Carew (Sir George's daughter), Dr. Jekyll pulls away from the dancer and flees the club.

So how did Dr. Jekyll fall and give birth to Mr. Hyde?

Dr. Jekyll fell when he allowed the torment of feeling inferior and insecure open up a dialogue between his good nature and the impulses of his lust:

Back at home, Dr. Jekyll sits in his library with his face in his hands. And for the first time in his life, Dr. Jekyll was awakened to a sense of his darker nature.

As he sat in his lounge chair, the wheels in his mind turned and turned. He was searching for answers on how to suffice the lustful calls that engrossed his being without losing his true self.

The dialogue between his good nature and his lusts created a new idea:

All of a sudden an epiphany occurs, "Wouldn't it be marvelous if the two natures of man could be housed in two different bodies?"

The purpose of this new idea was to counter and repair the damage Sir George's opinions had caused. So Dr. Jekyll uses the faculty of thought to invent an instrument that would allow his new idea to take flight and give power to a stronger personality:

He takes his epiphany and applies science to it. The result: a potion...a potion that could release the savage in him while keeping his true identity a secret. Thus Mr. Hyde was born.

When Dr. Jekyll drinks his special potion he transforms into a hideous replica of himself, Mr. Hyde. Hyde immediately goes back to the gentlemen's club and convinces the club owner to set up a private meeting with the same dancer that enticed his counterpart, Dr. Jekyll. But her company didn't quench Hyde's lustful thirst. So he continued to hunt for the woman who could.

Hyde grew even more evil by adding heavy drinking to

the mix, which ultimately caused him to become violent and abrasive.

Hyde's acts of rape, debauchery, and drunkenness caused the death of a good man. For in the end, Hyde was tracked down by the police to Dr. Jekyll's lab and shot. As Hyde falls to the floor, the form of a lifeless Dr. Jekyll reappears.

As our biblical text states, we must police what we are thinking. Failure to do so could very well set our lives on a collision course toward a horrible end.

Who's Talking: The Good, the Bad, or the Ugly?

Individual lifestyle is built upon an original idea(s) that leads to or produces a particular outcome. For example, philanthropy was the idea of origin that led Dr. Jekyll to a lifestyle of medical scientific research for the betterment of mankind. Mr. Hyde was born from the same premise; lust was the idea of origin, and rape and drunkenness was the outcome.

The energy that moves an original idea(s) to a particular outcome (preferences, prejudices, personality, aspirations, habits, emotions, etc.) is dialogue.

Original Idea → Dialogue → Outcome

Dialogue is the instrument that the faculty of thought uses to:

1. *Decipher questions*—the interrogation process of an original idea, outside opinion, suggestion, or personal observation
    a. To discern what, when, where, why, and how
2. *Find relevancy*—the study of an original idea and its possible outcomes for personal knowledge of whether the possibilities of an original idea are beneficial or detrimental to one's well-being
3. *Contemplate actions*—envision a plan of direction and the implementation of its construction, maintenance, and/or management of the expedition to experience what our study has discovered

In essence, we "talk" to ourselves. We converse with what we are thinking or feeling in order to navigate through everyday life.

On my continuous journey to be the best of who God has predestined me to be, I have discovered that there are three types of inner personal dialogue: the Good, the Bad, and the Ugly. My discovery of how to discern "who's talking" has created for me a vantage point of making better decisions, instituting plans with clearer direction, and implementing a more effective process of managing my feelings and desires.

My goal for the rest of this chapter is to define each form of inner personal dialogue so that you can create for yourself a vantage point over the Hyde that may be lurking in the shadows of your own conscious.

The Good

> Come now, and let us reason together, saith the LORD: though your sins be as scarlet, they shall be

as white as snow; though they be red like crimson, they shall be as wool.

—ISAIAH 1:18

I believe that humanity is God's original idea (Gen. 1:26–28).

I also believe that God blesses every individual that is born with a specific purpose (Rom. 8:29–30), or what I call a unique God-given brand.

I believe that the Bible is God's manufacturer's manual that provides resources for each individual's unique brand. The manual reveals truths, options, real-life examples, maintenance, management, reconciliation processes for both human relationships and a relationship with the divine, strategies on how to handle enemies, and reconstruction methods to ensure successful implementation of each person's unique God-given brand.

Therefore, I believe that the best and most efficient energy necessary to move a person into his or her destiny is *dialogue with God*.

I believe we have all heard God's voice before, but have oftentimes defined His voice as our own conscience. This doesn't exclude individual ethics nor does it minimize a person's inherent good nature, because we are all built with the capacity to sense right or wrong.

However, I believe that every good gift and every perfect gift comes from God (James 1:17). And I believe that being able to tell the difference between personal ethics and divine institution will strengthen our ability to decipher and employ what is best for our lives.

I believe that whenever you or I are at the crossroad of determination, God takes the time to speak to us (Rev. 3:20). "For what purpose?" you ask. God takes the time to talk to us whenever we are at the crossroads of determination because He desires to guide us to the destiny that is best suited for our unique brand of talents and gifts.

Even still, the choice will always be ours to either listen to and follow God's GPS or our own. If you do not want His advice, God will respect your choice (even though He may be disappointed that you didn't) and let you go your way.

His love for you and me never dissipates. He will always be at the door of our hearts waiting for us to let Him in.

And if we are willing to discuss with God, our architect, what we envision for our lives and compare it with what He has originally designed, then we can position ourselves into a prosperous partnership with infinite possibilities.

So how can we recognize when God is speaking? I believe we can begin to recognize God's voice when we intimately and willingly familiarize ourselves with all three persons of His character: God the Father, God the Son (Jesus Christ), and God the Holy Spirit. I believe that each is different but all make up the one true God. Here are the basics:

1. The Father
   a. He is the leader of the three (Matt. 6:9–13; 2 Cor. 1:3; Eph. 4:6). His voice is laced with an authoritative or fatherly tone. His expertise is in the principles of wisdom, truth, justice, character building, what is best, and what is right.
   b. He delights in spending time with His children. He will draw you and me to Him and reveal His heart. We mean the world to Him, and it shows when He speaks to us.

    c. His love for us drives Him to give us provision, protection, and purpose. The Father's love also drives Him to chasten us when we do wrong. The Father will hold His children accountable for their actions and will graciously take the time to lead them to restoration.

    d. The Father is an encourager of the concept, "To be something you have to do something." In essence, He encourages us to be responsible, humble, trustworthy, decisive, intelligent, wise, calculating, and strategic.

2. The Son

    a. Jesus Christ is the right hand of the Father (Mark 16:19; Heb. 1:3). He promotes the adherence to the principles the Father sets (Matt. 12:50; John 14:23). He is the example or criterion for what it means to be human and how that definition relates to being an heir of the kingdom of God and a child of the Father (Heb. 4:14–16).

    b. His voice is very compassionate. His love is unconditional and His ability to hear and see us for who we are is extraordinary.

    c. His love is beyond measure. He cares for us, empathizes with our heartaches and failures, gives comfort when we need it most, and will break with force whatever may hold us bound (Matt. 11:28–30; John 8:36).

    d. His expertise is intercession between humanity and the Father, rectifying dysfunctions of the human condition, forgiveness, compassion, understanding, producing rest and peace, sin and burden bearing, inspiration, encouragement, grace, and mercy.

    e. The Son is an encourager of the concept, "You can." He inspires each of us to believe that nothing is impossible and that we all possess gifts or talents of great worth.

3. The Holy Spirit

    a. The Holy Spirit is the "hand" of God that advocates the principles of the Father (John 14:26) and affirms the work of the Son (John 15:26). His voice is that of a teacher and a guide.

    b. His expertise is confirming the reality of the Father and the Son, worship, fulfilling the promises of both the Father and the Son, communication management between the natural and the spiritual, adversity management, empowerment of each believer, giver of wisdom and revelation, guidance, and the proprietor of deliverance and healing.

    c. He is the signature of the very presence of God both universally and within each believer.

    d. The Holy Spirit reassures us that the Father and the Son will keep their word and, when necessary, will speak on our behalf of any concerns we may have that we may not be able to verbalize completely to the Father or to the Son (Rom. 8:26–27).

Now that we know the basics, let's go to an example of God speaking at the crossroad of individual determination:

> One day Moses was tending the flock of his father-in-law, Jethro, the priest of Midian. He led the flock far into the wilderness and came to Sinai, the mountain of God. There the angel of the LORD appeared to him in a blazing fire from the middle of a bush. Moses stared in amazement. Though the bush was engulfed in flames, it didn't burn up. "This is amazing," Moses said to himself. "Why isn't that bush burning up? I must go see it."
> —EXODUS 3:1–3, NLT

Raised as an adopted son of Pharaoh, Moses's current situation wasn't by choice but by necessity. You see, Moses was a wanted killer. He had murdered an Egyptian slave master for severely beating a Hebrew slave.

Fearful of what would happen, Moses fled Egypt into the land of Midian.

In Midian, Moses settled into a new life. He married the daughter of Jethro, the priest of Midian, and joined the family business of sheep herding.

As years passed, Moses began to show signs of discontent. He led his flock further out into the wilderness than normal and ended up at Mt. Sinai, the mountain where the Midianites believed God resided.

It was as if Moses was searching for something.

Our text hints at the fact that God sees that Moses is searching for something and decides to get his attention with a burning bush. God waits patiently for Moses to further investigate the bush before speaking:

> When the LORD saw Moses coming to take a closer look, God called to him from the middle of the bush, "Moses! Moses!" "Here I am!" Moses replied. "Do not come any closer," the LORD warned. "Take off your sandals, for you are

standing on holy ground. I am the God of your father—the God of Abraham, the God of Isaac, and the God of Jacob." When Moses heard this, he covered his face because he was afraid to look at God.

—Exodus 3:4–6, nlt

The Father is the first to speak. He calls to Moses and draws him closer with the burning bush so that they could talk.

In verse five, the Holy Spirit speaks. He sets the stage for an intimate conversation by teaching Moses a simple form of worship: *"Take off your sandals, for you are standing on holy ground."*

Once the stage is set, the Father speaks again and introduces everyone to Moses: *"I am the God of your father— the God of Abraham, the God of Isaac, and the God of Jacob."*

Now that the Father has broken the ice, the Son speaks:

> Then the Lord told him, "I have certainly seen the oppression of my people in Egypt. I have heard their cries of distress because of their harsh slave drivers. Yes, I am aware of their suffering. So I have come down to rescue them from the power of the Egyptians and lead them out of Egypt into their own fertile and spacious land.
>
> —Exodus 3:7–8, nlt

The Son empathizes with Moses. He understood the heartache Moses felt when he saw the slave master severely beating a fellow Hebrew.

The Son also compassionately forgives Moses for his wrongdoing. As if to answer Moses's guilt, the Son says, "Yes, I am aware of their suffering. So I have come down to rescue them from the power of the Egyptians and lead them out of Egypt."

Now I have to pause here for a moment. God's way of speaking is very different from ours (Isa. 55:8). His language is based in symbolism and analogy. The purpose for speaking in this manner is to invoke the faculty of thought within the mind of whom He speaks to. God's style of communicating:

1. Reveals truth hidden from the natural eye or perspective
2. Teaches what needs to be understood in a format that will produce wisdom
3. Exposes the source(s) of an individual's character flaws and how to fix them
4. Provides discernment of people, situations, problems, etc.
5. Institutes true love and compassion
6. Restores, rebuilds, and rejuvenates
7. Gives direction
8. Alarms of danger and the need to change direction
9. Gives hope and encouragement
10. Provides strategy and methodology
11. Sets the stage for an individual to freely make an educated decision

God is a thinker. So His approach to life is from a thinker's perspective. I believe God had the Bible written in various styles by various intellects in order to set aflame our mind's ability to reason, calculate, adapt, discover, deconstruct, reconstruct, or create in a broad number of subject matter. It is for this reason that Proverbs 4 admonishes us to get wisdom because wisdom is the principle by which all other things exist.

I also believe that God specializes in relevancy. Relevancy is the fuel to understanding and the inspiration to commit to that understanding.

Relevancy doesn't corrupt truth but makes it digestible even when the truth hurts. So when the Son tells Moses, *"I am aware of their suffering,"* He was identifying with both Moses's past transgression and the children of Israel's current plight. The Son's implication of *"rescuing them from the power of the Egyptians"* was a reference to the salvation for both Moses and the children of Israel.

Once Moses's salvation was established by the Son, the Father gave Moses his predestined purpose:

> "Look! The cry of the people of Israel has reached me, and I have seen how harshly the Egyptians abuse them. Now go, for I am sending you to Pharaoh. You must lead my people Israel out of Egypt."
>
> —Exodus 3:9–10, NLT

It was no coincidence that Moses was raised as an Egyptian prince. God placed Moses in Egypt as a child so that he could learn the Egyptian culture and psyche. Moses's experience as an Egyptian prince gave him the skills necessary to not only negotiate his fellow Hebrews' release but the ability to govern them as well. His action against the Egyptian slave master may have been overzealous but revealed the true passions of his heart to make a difference in his Hebrew brethren's lives.

But when it came down to his God-given brand, Moses wasn't easily convinced:

> But Moses protested to God, "Who am I to appear before Pharaoh? Who am I to lead the people of Israel out of Egypt?"
> —Exodus 3:11, NLT

In Exodus 3:11–22 and 4:1–8, God and Moses discuss his purpose and destiny. Moses poses questions, fears, and concerns, and God patiently answers each and reassures Moses by revealing His power.

But the trauma of Moses's past makes him fearful and insecure about his God-given brand:

> But Moses pleaded with the Lord, "O Lord, I'm not very good with words. I never have been, and I'm not now, even though you have spoken to me. I get tongue-tied, and my words get tangled." Then the Lord asked Moses, "Who makes a person's mouth? Who decides whether people speak or do not speak, hear or do not hear, see or do not see? Is it not I, the Lord? Now go! I will be with you as you speak, and I will instruct you in what to say."
> But Moses again pleaded, "Lord, please! Send anyone else."
> —Exodus 4:10–13, NLT

In Exodus 4:14, the Father gets angry with Moses. Remember the Father is an encourager of the concept *"to be something you have to do something,"* so seeing His son Moses's unwillingness to move forward in his God-given brand because of fear upset Him (just like any other parent who sees their child's unwillingness to make an effort to do something that they are more than capable of doing).

Love and compassion prevails, and the Father provides Moses with an option:

> "All right," he said. "What about your brother, Aaron the Levite? I know he speaks well. And look! He is on his way to meet you now. He will be delighted to see you. Talk to him, and put the words in his mouth. I will be with both of you as you speak, and I will instruct you both in what to do. Aaron will be your spokesman to the people. He will be your mouthpiece, and you will stand in the place of God for him, telling him what to say. And take your shepherd's staff with you, and use it to perform the miraculous signs I have shown you."
>
> —Exodus 4:14–17, NLT

Moses finds comfort with this added option. He accepts his God-given brand and becomes one of the most prominent men in history!

So, the next time you find yourself at the crossroads of determination, look for the "burning bush." It's your escape from mediocrity. It's your lifeline to finding the real you! Listen to that small, still voice seeking to get your attention and be open-minded to the positives it suggests and the realities of your situation it reveals.

The Bad

> The thief's purpose is to steal and kill and destroy.
> —John 10:10, NLT

> For they that are after the flesh do mind the things of the flesh...For to be carnally minded

> is death...Because the carnal mind is enmity against God: for it is not subject to the law of God, neither indeed can be.
> — ROMANS 8:5–7

Humanity has been wonderfully and marvelously made. Our value in this universe is priceless and the expectations of our grandeur are without bounds.[2]

Because of such value, there are thieves in this world who seek to make use of that value for their own benefit; all the more reason for us to be careful of the company we keep and the type of information we intake.

It is safe to say that having dialogue with the thief is oftentimes the energy that leads to the birth of our darker selves. Examples of this are found in Adam and Eve's conversation with the serpent (Satan) and Dr. Jekyll's conversation with Sir George Carew.

In any case, bad behavior is learned behavior that is often introduced to us by some type of outside influence, environment, or social structure.

However, although we may be able to track the thief's influence(s) on our vices, habits, flaws, relationships, preferences, prejudices, or beliefs, we must take into account and be responsible for our own actions.

The release of our dark side is undoubtedly the product of caving in to our own lusts (James 1:14–15). The apostle Paul calls this "minding the flesh" (Rom. 8:5). Such submission often leads to a sinful lifestyle.

Now I must say that sin is another idea that has been lost in translation. Our legalistic or lackadaisical view of sin and the corrupt implementation of condemning those who have sinned has left many of us frustrated and lost.

The religious system(s) has left those of us who need God the most offended and angry.

I believe Jesus gives us a very simple definition of what sin is and an example of how *we* can become the instrument that gives life to our dark side:

> "A man had two sons. The younger son told his father, 'I want my share of your estate now before you die.' So his father agreed to divide his wealth between his sons."
> —Luke 15:11–12, NLT

Unto every person that is born, God freely gives a share of His estate (Ps. 24:1–2; Gen. 1:28–30; Eph. 1:11). What we do with that inheritance is up to us.

> A few days later this younger son packed all his belongings and moved to a distant land, and there he wasted all his money in wild living.
> —Luke 15:13, NLT

Sin is the deliberate or yielding choice to lusts, wastefulness, recklessness, greed, selfishness, intellectual conceit, malicious intent against others, or misplaced affections.

Most of our sinful acts aren't even against God directly. They are mainly acts against ourselves.

> About the time his money ran out, a great famine swept over the land, and he began to starve. He persuaded a local farmer to hire him, and the man sent him into his fields to feed the pigs.
>
> The young man became so hungry that even the pods he was feeding the pigs looked good to him. But no one gave him anything.
> —Luke 15:14–16, NLT

It is the fruit that sin bears that stirs God's hatred against it.

It pains God to have to sit and watch His children self-destruct or become poisonous to the universal family as a whole:

> The LORD observed the extent of human wickedness on the earth, and he saw that everything they thought or imagined was consistently and totally evil. So the LORD was sorry he had ever made them and put them on the earth. It broke his heart.
> —GENESIS 6:5–6, NLT

That's why God sets standards for His children with the expectation that they will follow.

Obedience to the standards of God is a love principle (John 14:23). It's about complying to the desires of someone who has your best interest at heart and someone you greatly love, respect, honor, and enjoy (as a child should obey his/her mom and dad, or a husband who should assent to the heart of his wife, or a wife who should surrender to the desires of her husband, or friends who respect the bond that they share).

Disobedience, on the other hand, is a binding principle. It shackles us to the dysfunctions born from our sins. Such dysfunction causes a strain on the love relationship with God and amongst each other, and in many cases can completely sever such relationships.

Take the younger son in the parable of the prodigal son for an example. His choice of lifestyle separated him from the covering of his father's love and the benefits his father provided. It pushed him over the edge until he hit rock bottom, where no one cared for him or had any desire to help him (Luke 15:15–16).

It wasn't until the younger son recognized he had

hit rock bottom that he was able to make a more viable decision:

> When he finally came to his senses, he said to himself, "At home even the hired servants have food enough to spare, and here I am dying of hunger! I will go home to my father and say, 'Father, I have sinned against both heaven and you, and I am no longer worthy of being called your son. Please take me on as a hired servant.'"
> —LUKE 15:17–19, NLT

It was the younger son's admission to his mistakes and his willingness to change and comply with what he felt was best for him (his father's standards) that improved his situation.

What Jesus emphasizes next is what we all need to see and remember:

> So he returned home to his father. And while he was still a long way off, his father saw him coming. Filled with love and compassion, he ran to his son, embraced him, and kissed him. His son said to him, "Father, I have sinned against both heaven and you, and I am no longer worthy of being called your son."
>
> But his father said to the servants, "Quick! Bring the finest robe in the house and put it on him. Get a ring for his finger and sandals for his feet. And kill the calf we have been fattening. We must celebrate with a feast, for this son of mine was dead and has now returned to life. He was lost, but now he is found." So the party began.
> —LUKE 15:20–24, NLT

Jesus shows that God seeks to celebrate, reward, and protect His children, not condemn them (Rom. 8:1). All we have to do is learn how not to condemn ourselves or each other.[3]

Now that we have defined the Bad, let's explore an example and get a closer look of how it can affect our destiny.

In the Book of Judges, a hero was born:

> In those days a man named Manoah from the tribe of Dan lived in the town of Zorah. His wife was unable to become pregnant, and they had no children. The angel of the LORD appeared to Manoah's wife and said, "Even though you have been unable to have children, you will soon become pregnant and give birth to a son. So be careful; you must not drink wine or any other alcoholic drink nor eat any forbidden food. You will become pregnant and give birth to a son, and his hair must never be cut. For he will be dedicated to God as a Nazirite from birth. He will begin to rescue Israel from the Philistines."...
>
> When her son was born, she named him Samson. And the LORD blessed him as he grew up. And the Spirit of the LORD began to stir him while he lived in Mahaneh-dan, which is located between the towns of Zorah and Eshtaol.
> —JUDGES 13:2–5, 24–25, NLT

Samson's God-given brand was to save Israel from their Philistine oppressors. God's plan for Samson to accomplish this goal I believe is found in Judges 14:1–4 (NLT):

> One day when Samson was in Timnah, one of the Philistine women caught his eye. When he returned home, he told his father and mother, "A

young Philistine woman in Timnah caught my eye. I want to marry her. Get her for me."

His father and mother objected. "Isn't there even one woman in our tribe or among all the Israelites you could marry?" they asked. "Why must you go to the pagan Philistines to find a wife?"

But Samson told his father, "Get her for me! She looks good to me." His father and mother didn't realize the LORD was at work in this, creating an opportunity to work against the Philistines, who ruled over Israel at that time.

I believe that God desired to end the conflict between Israel and the Philistines peaceably. To be "against" something or someone isn't always a negative endeavor. In this case I believe the word *against* means "to protect from."

I believe God was planning to use marriage as the instrument to protect Israel from further torment at the hands of the Philistines and at the same time show mercy *upon* the Philistines.

History has dictated that many conflicts between two cultures have been rectified by the marriage between opposing royal families. In this case no royalty was involved but the principle was the same. As a matter of fact, God used this method with the marriage between Esther, a beautiful Jewish woman, and King Ahasuerus of Persia to save Israel from Haman, a Persian dignitary who plotted to exterminate them.

Samson was the epitome of masculine stature. He was blessed by God with incredible strength (Judg. 14:5–7). Such a man could gain the respect of his enemies and could therefore peaceably solve a volatile situation (Judg. 14:10–11).

God's plan was going well until the night of Samson's "bachelor party":

> Samson said to them, "Let me tell you a riddle. If you solve my riddle during these seven days of the celebration, I will give you thirty fine linen robes and thirty sets of festive clothing. But if you can't solve it, then you must give me thirty fine linen robes and thirty sets of festive clothing."
> "All right," they agreed, "let's hear your riddle."
> —JUDGES 14:12–13, NLT

Samson's gamble put more strain on an already extremely tense situation. Neither of these cultures knew how to get along. The marriage was supposed to allow each side to get to know one another in a more amicable light. But when money is involved, you can expect some drama:

> Three days later they were still trying to figure it out. On the fourth day they said to Samson's wife, "Entice your husband to explain the riddle for us, or we will burn down your father's house with you in it. Did you invite us to this party just to make us poor?"
> So Samson's wife came to him in tears and said, "You don't love me; you hate me! You have given my people a riddle, but you haven't told me the answer."
> "I haven't even given the answer to my father or mother," he replied. "Why should I tell you?" So she cried whenever she was with him and kept it up for the rest of the celebration. At last, on the seventh day he told her the answer because she was tormenting him with her nagging. Then she explained the riddle to the young men.
> So before sunset of the seventh day, the men

of the town came to Samson with their answer: "What is sweeter than honey? What is stronger than a lion?"

Samson replied, "If you hadn't plowed with my heifer, you wouldn't have solved my riddle!"

Then the Spirit of the LORD came powerfully upon him. He went down to the town of Ashkelon, killed thirty men, took their belongings, and gave their clothing to the men who had solved his riddle. Samson was furious about what had happened, and he went back home to live with his father and mother. So his wife was given in marriage to the man who had been Samson's best man at the wedding.
—JUDGES 14:14–20, NLT

We often make the mistake of believing that the phrase "the Spirit of the Lord came powerfully upon him" as an indication that God was ordaining Samson's actions. But in reality the phrase was only a confirmation of the gift God had entrusted Samson to possess.

In Christ's parable of the prodigal son, we've learned that God gives each of us an inheritance. What we do with that inheritance is up to us. So when the text says that "the Spirit of the Lord came powerfully upon him," it identified Samson's inheritance from God. What he did with it was his choice.

Samson chose to use his God-given strength to rob and murder thirty innocent men so that he could pay off his gambling debt to the young Philistine men that were at his "bachelor's party" (Judg. 14:19).

God's original plan to bring peace between Israel and the Philistines was now in jeopardy because of Samson's sinful behavior. But who do you think Samson's sin hurt the most? Samson, of course:

> Later on, during the wheat harvest, Samson took a young goat as a present to his wife. He said, "I'm going into my wife's room to sleep with her," but her father wouldn't let him in.
>
> "I truly thought you must hate her," her father explained, "so I gave her in marriage to your best man. But look, her younger sister is even more beautiful than she is. Marry her instead."
>
> —JUDGES 15:1–2, NLT

Samson's gambling was the sin that opened the door to the "Hyde" in him. The apostle Paul describes this as carnal thinking (Rom. 8:6).

Once Mr. Hyde is released it is very difficult to contain him:

> Samson said, "This time I cannot be blamed for everything I am going to do to you Philistines." Then he went out and caught 300 foxes. He tied their tails together in pairs, and he fastened a torch to each pair of tails. Then he lit the torches and let the foxes run through the grain fields of the Philistines. He burned all their grain to the ground, including the sheaves and the uncut grain. He also destroyed their vineyards and olive groves.
>
> —JUDGES 15:3–5, NLT

Instead of Samson becoming an instrument of peace, by choice he became an instrument of destruction. He not only had become harmful to himself but to his fellow man:

> The Philistines retaliated by setting up camp in Judah and spreading out near the town of Lehi. The men of Judah asked the Philistines, "Why are you attacking us?" The Philistines replied, "We've

Think About What You're Thinking

> come to capture Samson. We've come to pay him back for what he did to us." So 3,000 men of Judah went down to get Samson at the cave in the rock of Etam.
>
> They said to Samson, "Don't you realize the Philistines rule over us? What are you doing to us?" But Samson replied, "I only did to them what they did to me."
>
> —Judges 15:9–11, NLT

Samson was so engrossed in his own dysfunction that he was blind to what was really going on. He blamed the Philistines for *his* sins. It was Samson who chose to gamble, murder, steal, and vandalize. Samson's carnal thinking now had his life spiraling into chaos. Like we mentioned earlier in this chapter, if your thoughts are out of whack your life will be out of whack as well.

However, God still had faith in him and showed mercy upon him:

> Samson was now very thirsty, and he cried out to the Lord, "You have accomplished this great victory by the strength of your servant. Must I now die of thirst and fall into the hands of these pagans?" So God caused water to gush out of a hollow in the ground at Lehi, and Samson was revived as he drank.
>
> —Judges 15:18–19, NLT

But Samson continued to misuse his gift:

> One day Samson went to the Philistine town of Gaza and spent the night with a prostitute. Word soon spread that Samson was there, so the men of Gaza gathered together and waited all night at the town gates. They kept quiet during the night,

saying to themselves, "When the light of morning comes, we will kill him."

But Samson stayed in bed only until midnight. Then he got up, took hold of the doors of the town gate, including the two posts, and lifted them up, bar and all. He put them on his shoulders and carried them all the way to the top of the hill across from Hebron.

—JUDGES 16:1–3 , NLT

Samson's carnal or Hyde-like thinking was not only adversely affecting his own life but also God's plan for the lives of the children of Israel and the lives of the Philistines (the people that God wanted to save). The apostle Paul describes this as "enmity" or antagonism or hostility against God. It got to the point where God made it clear that enough was enough:

Finally, Samson shared his secret with her. "My hair has never been cut," he confessed, "for I was dedicated to God as a Nazirite from birth. If my head were shaved, my strength would leave me, and I would become as weak as anyone else."

Delilah realized he had finally told her the truth, so she sent for the Philistine rulers. "Come back one more time," she said, "for he has finally told me his secret." So the Philistine rulers returned with the money in their hands. Delilah lulled Samson to sleep with his head in her lap, and then she called in a man to shave off the seven locks of his hair. In this way she began to bring him down, and his strength left him.

Then she cried out, "Samson! The Philistines have come to capture you!" When he woke up, he thought, "I will do as before and shake myself free." But he didn't realize the LORD had left him.

So the Philistines captured him and gouged out his eyes. They took him to Gaza, where he was bound with bronze chains and forced to grind grain in the prison.

—JUDGES 16:17–21, NLT

Like the prodigal son, Samson had wasted his inheritance with riotous living and was now in a "pigpen" situation. Samson had hit rock bottom and was now reaping the harvest of submitting to his dark side.

Here is an example of why we stress the importance of repentance. No one—and I mean no one—wants to find themselves at rock bottom. But if it happens, the best way out is to take responsibility for your actions and work your way out. Take charge and use the gifts God has given you to turn things around before it's too late:

> The Philistine rulers held a great festival, offering sacrifices and praising their god, Dagon. They said, "Our god has given us victory over our enemy Samson!" When the people saw him, they praised their god, saying, "Our god has delivered our enemy to us! The one who killed so many of us is now in our power!"
>
> Half-drunk by now, the people demanded, "Bring out Samson so he can amuse us!" So he was brought from the prison to amuse them, and they had him stand between the pillars supporting the roof.
>
> Samson said to the young servant who was leading him by the hand, "Place my hands against the pillars that hold up the temple. I want to rest against them." Now the temple was completely

filled with people. All the Philistine rulers were there, and there were about 3,000 men and women on the roof who were watching as Samson amused them.

Then Samson prayed to the LORD, "Sovereign Lord, remember me again. O God, please strengthen me just one more time. With one blow let me pay back the Philistines for the loss of my two eyes." Then Samson put his hands on the two center pillars that held up the temple. Pushing against them with both hands, he prayed, "Let me die with the Philistines." And the temple crashed down on the Philistine rulers and all the people. So he killed more people when he died than he had during his entire lifetime.

—JUDGES 16:23–30, NLT

It's sad. As gifted as Samson was, he never reached his full potential. He wreaked more havoc than good. He was the judge (chosen savior) of Israel for twenty years but could neither completely deliver Israel out of the Philistines' tormenting hands nor positively represent his God-given brand.

Even at the end of his life he never repented of any wrongdoing. And as seen in this text, his death came by his own hands; just like Dr. Jekyll.

As believers we could be biased and think that his death (which also brought death to many Philistines) worked out for the good of Israel. But what about the Philistines whom God sought to show mercy? Remember, God wishes that *no man* should perish (2 Pet. 3:9)! Most importantly, God wants those of us who call ourselves His servants to think and behave accordingly:

> Brethren, if a man be overtaken in a fault, ye which are spiritual, restore such an one in the spirit of meekness; considering thyself, lest thou also be tempted.
> —GALATIANS 6:1

We must not make the mistake of using the principle "all things work together for their good" improperly.

For example, there is an undeniable contrast between Joseph (Gen. 30:24–50:2) and Samson (Judg. 14–16:30). Joseph's struggles didn't come from bad choices but from haters and naysayers (Gen. 37:3–28; 39:7–11). Joseph rose to excellence because he used his God-given brand productively (Gen. 39:1–4; 22; 41:25–44). Israel was able to survive a seven-year famine because of Joseph's God-given brand that was perfected by his triumphs over every trial and tribulation he had been through. In Joseph's case, the principle "all things work together for their good" applies.

Samson's journey, however, was marked by one bad decision after the other. He blindly believed that his actions were the will of God. As a matter of fact, the apostle Paul had the same problem. Paul persecuted and killed many Christians in the name of God. It wasn't until he met Jesus on the road to Damascus that he saw that his faith was misplaced and misguided and was causing more harm to the people of God then good (Acts 9:1–20).

Samson's faith that helped him "close the mouths of lions" (Heb. 11:32–33) was corrupted by his sinful escapades. His lack of desire to repent halted his ability to turn things around and do better.

If Samson would have repented of his actions, then the principle "all things work together for their good" would apply (2 Chron. 7:14). Samson could have learned from his mistakes and may have had the opportunity to mend what he had broken. But that didn't happen.

Samson's bad boy behavior brought Israel and the Philistines together temporarily, but only because they both shared a common enemy, Samson (Judg. 15:9–11).

So Samson became Israel's instrument of peace, but not in a good sense. Therefore, the principle "all things work together for their good" doesn't apply.

However, there is one principle that does apply, and that's "the wages of sin is death" (Rom. 6:23, 8:6). Samson's reckless behavior caught up with him and he ended up failing God, himself, and his people; the same can happen to you or me.[4]

The Ugly

> Deeper and deeper I sink into the mire; I can't find a foothold. I am in deep water, and the floods overwhelm me. I am exhausted from crying for help; my throat is parched. My eyes are swollen with weeping.
> —PSALM 69:2–3A, NLT

Is every unfortunate, tragic, disconcerting, or heartbreaking situation born from sin? No. Some of these circumstances occur because of an assumption, or a misinterpretation, or a misunderstanding:

> The simple inherit folly: but the prudent are crowned with knowledge.
> —PROVERBS 14:18

And in some cases, things just happen:

> As Jesus was walking along, he saw a man who had been blind from birth. "Rabbi," his disciples

asked him, "why was this man born blind? Was it because of his own sins or his parents' sins?"

"It was not because of his sins or his parents' sins," Jesus answered. "This happened so the power of God could be seen in him."

—JOHN 9:1–3, NLT

In any case, we all have to deal with the Ugly that tribulation leaves behind.

So what is the Ugly? The Ugly can be categorized into three sections: family dysfunction, trauma, and addiction.

Family Dysfunction

I stated earlier in this chapter that humanity is God's original idea (Gen. 1:26–28). He blesses every individual that is born with a specific purpose, or what I call a unique God-given brand. However, each individual brand is connected to a unit (family) which also carries its own brand.

Each family unit has specific traits that signify its identity and are passed down from generation to generation.

Individual dysfunction is inherently dependent upon the dynamic that is present within that individual's family unit. Take Cain, for example. His individual malfunction can be linked to his mom and dad's dysfunction of the blame game (Gen. 3:12–13; 4:2–10).

That being said, whether a person comes from a good home or a broken one, a good number of their character flaws can be traced back to some type of family dysfunction that derives from one or all of these areas:

1. *Discipline*—Lack of a positive balanced system of correction and instruction
    a. Correction was either harsh and inflexible or too lenient and lackadaisical

b. Instruction was either manipulative and controlling or degrading and condemning or altogether absent
2. *Expression*—One's thoughts or feelings are disregarded, quenched, or misguided, which can:
   a. Disrupt an individual's ability to decipher one's personal identity
   b. Corrupt an individual's perception of one's identity, gifts, talents, purpose
   c. Turn the individual into a replica of the family brand versus an extension or innovation of the family franchise.
3. *Interaction*—A family's failure to embrace, support, or provide positive reinforcement on an intimate level with each other.
   a. Individuals suffer because of family disarray due to:
      i. Constant arguing or fighting
      ii. Verbal abuse
      iii. Condescension or condemnation of one's character
      iv. Exploitation of one's vulnerabilities
      v. Being used as a punching bag for other family member's frustrations
      vi. Lack of affection or attention
      vii. Treated as a burden or hindrance to another's happiness or fulfillment

Trauma

Just as dialogue is the energy that moves an original idea(s) to a particular outcome, trauma is the energy that moves an original idea(s) or experience to a particular dysfunction.

original idea or experience → trauma → particular dysfunction

A person's overall well-being can be harmfully affected by traumatic events such as:

1. Unexpected or abrupt situations

2. Negative thoughts, low perspective of esteem

3. Abrasive or confrontational conversations that challenge or cause injury to one's perspective of life

4. Judgmental or defacing comments about one's character

5. Verbal or physical abuse; victim of rumor or gossip, bullying, rape, incest, domestic violence, etc.

6. Tragedy

7. Embarrassing moments

8. Loneliness

9. Breakup of a significant relationship

10. Family dysfunction

11. Disease or physical injury

12. Fear

Dysfunction is often the result of a person's inability to psychologically, emotionally, or physically cope or recover from a traumatic event(s). An example of this principle was apparent in Dr. Jekyll's dilemma:

1. Dr. Jekyll experienced psychological trauma during his conversation with Sir George Carew. The conversation injured his idea of helping others and gave birth to an identity crisis.
2. The identity crisis caused trauma to Dr. Jekyll's emotions.
    a. Low self-worth and insecurity overwhelmed him and enabled Dr. Jekyll's growing dysfunction of identity confusion to latch on to Sir George Carew's idea of *"A man cannot destroy the savage in him by denying its impulses. The only way to get rid of temptation is to yield to it!"*
3. Dr. Jekyll's identity crisis and emotional trauma caused him to give in to going into an environment (gentlemen's club) that was dangerous to his true identity and feelings.
    a. Dr. Jekyll's submission to the environment at the gentlemen's club induced a physically traumatic experience.
        i. Lust for the dancer was so insatiable that Dr. Jekyll was beside himself; as he sat in his lounge chair, the wheels in his mind turned and turned. He was searching for

answers on how to suffice the lustful calls that engrossed his being without losing his true self.
  ii. This drove Dr. Jekyll to self-medicate with addiction. All of a sudden an epiphany occurs: "Wouldn't it be marvelous if the two natures of man could be housed in two different bodies?" He takes his epiphany and applies science to it. The result: a potion—a potion that could release the savage in him while keeping his true identity a secret. Thus Mr. Hyde was born.
4. The Mr. Hyde persona became the instrument and outward reality of Dr. Jekyll's psychological, emotional, and physical trauma.

Remember, thoughts are the building blocks of principles that evaluate and commission a perspective of life wherein our feelings find validity and our choices receive direction. So a person's inability to cope or recover from the stress of a traumatic event can cause one's thoughts to malfunction to the point where neither their emotions can find validation nor can their will find healthy direction.

Therefore it is imperative that we investigate any trauma that may exist in our lives, whether the trauma was caused by falling into the trap of the thief, our own sin, or by tribulation.

Addiction

Family dysfunction and trauma can force a person to find a counterbalance(s) to relieve the negative effects each may have on his/her life. The unfortunate reality is the counterbalance(s) is oftentimes an enabler to even more harmful dysfunctions.

There are three categories of addiction:

1. *Tolerance*: The management of pain or discomfort.
   a. A person that continues to subconsciously experience a physical traumatic event (although the injuries sustained by the event have passed) and uses various substances for relief
   b. The use of substances for relief of psychological and emotional trauma from physical injuries sustained from severe accidents or assault (rape, molestation, violence, etc.)
   c. A person who has developed a tolerance to a specific medication for relief of a predetermined condition and begins to increase their dosage uncontrollably
2. *Behavioral*: Compulsive and obsessive engagement in specific activities such as overeating, sex, exercise/sports, dieting, preservation of a certain body image, gambling, shopping, gossiping, bullying, hoarding, etc. Condition can be caused by:
   a. Sin
   b. Unresolved trauma
   c. Psychological or emotional condition or malfunction
3. *Dependency*: Overreliance on substances, a particular person, public opinion, etc. Condition can be:

a. Physical—body is addicted to a substance or experience; body reacts violently or disparagingly if dependency is cut off; withdrawal

b. Emotional—feelings are dependent upon affection from certain types of people at the expense of one's well-being; overbearing or obsessive feelings for a person, place, or thing to make up for the lack of personal validation.

c. Mental—the ability to function cognitively is determined by the intake of a substance, the perspective of certain types of people, or in severe cases, a sociopathic system of perspective

Transition

Throw off your old sinful nature and your former way of life, which is corrupted by lust and deception. Instead, let the Spirit renew your thoughts and attitudes. Put on your new nature, created to be like God—truly righteous and holy.
—Ephesians 4:22–24, NLT

One of the most difficult things for any of us to accomplish is *change*. Why? Because change demands that we leave our comfort zone(s) and venture out into the unknown.

Change requires that we leave the confines of the familiar, of what's easy, or what we think we know, and drive toward tough challenges, hard decisions, formidable obstacles, and the learning processes that produce what we *need* to know.

My friend, greatness isn't something that comes easy. You have to work for it. Better yet, you have to *fight* for it!

Hebrews 11:1 teaches that faith is the substance of those

things hoped for even when the evidence of those things isn't seen. One of the main reasons why many of us fall short of greatness is because we are too focused on what we see versus what we believe. Our hope has become conditional and can be easily swayed by various circumstances.

It is for this reason that I believe applying our Scripture text for this section is crucial to our transition from the ill effects of the Bad and the Ugly to the productivity and prosperity of the Good.

Our first step toward greatness is "throwing off" what may hold us down by reevaluating our current way of life and finding solutions and strategies that will help us to tear down any dysfunction that has been born from the Bad and the Ugly.

Therefore, we are going to have to look in the mirror and boldly confront Mr. Hyde face-to-face. We are going to have to have the guts to get rid of our intimate relationship with Mr. Hyde and the false securities he provides.

Most importantly, we are going to have to be willing to submit and commit to the fact that we're going to need help. We can't make the mistake of not seeking professional help from a doctor, life coach, or counselor because of our fear of what other people may think.

Second, we have to be motivated to change and aggressively let go of thoughts and feelings that can put us in unfavorable positions. We have to learn to think about what we are thinking and make adjustments accordingly so that our behavior will be favorable rather than unsavory.

My advice to you is reach out to God through Jesus Christ and *consistently learn* from His principles of how to think in a way that reflects the God-given brand that is within you. Remember, God seeks to invest in who you are and not condemn you. So when you learn of His standards, keep in mind that these standards are to bring out the best in you and to discard the garbage that is hurting you.

If some of you decide to go another way, apply the principle of changing how you think and feel. Find the mental and emotional garbage that is "stinking up" your life and get rid of it.

Third, put on that which is true, honest, and good. Just like putting new cabinets into a renovated kitchen, we have to "put on" compassion, faithfulness, abstinence, patience, longsuffering, love and kindness, strength, courage, temperance, and resourcefulness.

You can accomplish putting on these traits by investigating the meaning of each trait thoroughly and how to apply it.

Again, my friends, I believe just as our text states that we are able to put on these things through Christ Jesus. If we struggle with putting on these traits, He will give us a helping hand.

> And he said unto me, My grace is sufficient for thee: for my strength is made perfect in weakness. Most gladly therefore will I rather glory in my infirmities, that the power of Christ may rest upon me.
> —2 CORINTHIANS 12:9

No matter what you decide, we all have to stop beating ourselves up (along with everyone else) over our struggle with keeping our darker selves in check because it produces nothing but strife and barrenness.

Understand that God desires for every person to be holy, fair, and morally responsible just like He is; but know, my friend, that He grades how we implement these things on a learning curve called grace.

Our good standing before God is based on the grace that I believe was set by Jesus Christ's experience on earth as both human and divine (Rom. 5:1–5; Heb. 4:14–16). We are justified by His grace and have been given the opportunity to learn *how* to live holy, fair, and morally responsible lives (Prov. 4:5–9; Col. 3:1–3; 2 Tim. 2:15; 2 Pet. 1:2–8).

It is important that we all learn how to be gracious with ourselves and others. Know that it takes time to learn how to become something we've never been before, especially if you are considering giving Christ a try for the first time.

It's a blessing to know, my friends, that God will give us time to make better choices, to walk in the gifts and talents He has given us, and treat others with love and respect. He will hold us accountable for what we do (Gal. 6:7–8) and in the same instance give us ample time to fix what we have done (2 Cor. 12:9).

While facing various inadequacies that may exist in our lives, His grace will progress us from living defeated under the power of the Bad and the Ugly to living victorious *over* the Bad and the Ugly.

Finally, it is also important that we all learn how to forgive ourselves and others as God has forgiven us all (Mark 11:25). Jesus states in Matthew 18:21–22, we should forgive each other seventy times seven. In other words, we should continue to provide *complete* forgiveness to any offender no matter how many times he or she does it (especially if we are the offender).

But don't be naïve. God also admonishes us to use common sense:

> Give not that which is holy unto the dogs, neither cast ye your pearls before swine, lest they trample

them under their feet, and turn again and rend you.

—MATTHEW 7:6

Our heart is the essence of who we are. It is sacred and must be protected (Prov. 4:23). Forgiving an offender is one thing, but allowing that offender to continue to trample our heart is another.

Forgiveness is the instrument we can use to move on. It releases us from those who have offended or hurt us.

However, this doesn't mean that the offender will be less offensive. Some people will never change. Therefore, we have to be resilient enough to manage our heart in such a way that what they do or say no longer affects how we see ourselves or live our lives, and if necessary, remove or separate ourselves from being in contact with such people.[5]

So be bold. Show Mr. Hyde who's the boss!

Chapter Six
GOD'S PLAN, OUR VISION

> "Again, the Kingdom of Heaven can be illustrated by the story of a man going into another country, who called together his servants and loaned them money to invest for him while he was gone. He gave $5,000 to one, $2,000 to another, and $1,000 to the last—dividing it in proportion to their abilities."
> —Matthew 25:14–15, TLB

GOD GIVES EACH person specialized skills in proportion to each person's ability to manage and apply their gifts appropriately, which means some of us will be responsible for more gifts than others. It doesn't make us better than other people; just different.

No matter how much you have, if you manage and apply it well, God will give you more:

> "The man who received the $5,000 began immediately to buy and sell with it and soon earned another $5,000....After a long time their master returned from his trip and called them to him to account for his money. The man to whom he had entrusted the $5,000 brought him $10,000. His master praised him for good work. 'You have been faithful in handling this small amount,' he told him, 'so now I will give you many more responsibilities. Begin the joyous tasks I have assigned to you.'"
> —MATTHEW 25:16, 19–21, TLB

But if you waste or do nothing with what God gives you, He will give it to someone else:

> "The man who received $1,000 dug a hole in the ground and hid the money for safekeeping. After a long time their master returned from his trip and called them to him to account for his money....The man with the $1,000 came and said, 'Sir, I knew you were a hard man, and I was afraid you would rob me of what I earned, so I hid your money in the earth and here it is!'
>
> "But his master replied, 'Wicked man! Lazy slave! Since you knew I would demand your profit, you should at least have put my money into the bank so I could have some interest. Take the money from this man and give it to the man with the $10,000. For the man who uses well what he is given shall be given more, and he shall have

abundance. But from the man who is unfaithful, even what little responsibility he has shall be taken from him.'"
—MATTHEW 25:18–19, 24–29, TLB

This may not sit well with some of us. Maybe because some of us feel we are entitled to have versus acknowledging the fact that we are held accountable to earn. Always remember, my friends, to be something you have to do something. Doing nothing will only lead you to absolutely nothing!

So what kind of plan does God have for you or me?

Well, the basic plan that God calls all of us to participate in is making our world a better place (Gen. 1:27–28). He expects us to invest in each other and help each other that we all may enjoy life (Gal. 5:13).

God also chooses specific people to do specific things for specific purposes such as leading, governing, managing resources, training, engineering, designing, researching and discovering, imaginatively creating, entertaining, relating to others, administering, calculating, repairing, restoring, healing, building, growing, manufacturing, writing, inventing, investing, and protecting.

What I love about God the most is His fortitude in allowing you or me to envision *how* to accomplish and present what He chooses for us to do. Take Noah, for example. God gave him a specific plan and purpose for building an ark. The realization of that plan and its purpose was left up to Noah. It was Noah who had to envision the best location for construction of the ark, how to manage his resources effectively, calculate how much food and water to bring for a journey without a known expiration date, and how to collect two animals of every species. Today, that same freedom is true for you and me.

One of the most endearing plans I believe God provides is His permissive will. Within this plan, God takes the time to hear our opinion or desire of what we believe we can do with what He has given us. And if what we desire uses the gifts He's given us in a manner that is positive, constructive, and a blessing to others, He will give us the go-ahead.

Take Nehemiah, for example. He was the cupbearer for King Artaxerxes of Persia. One day his friend Hanani came to visit him. Nehemiah asked his friend how things were going in his hometown, Jerusalem. What he heard was disturbing. Nehemiah learned that his hometown was in great need of rebuilding, and he wanted to do something about it.

So Nehemiah asked God if He would help him ask King Artaxerxes if he could go back home and help rebuild his hometown. Not only did God give Nehemiah the courage to ask the king to allow him to leave for his hometown to rebuild it, but to also ask the king for official certifications and supplies to do so. King Artaxerxes granted Nehemiah's entire request! Nehemiah was able to rebuild his hometown physically, emotionally, and spiritually.

Whatever the plan and purpose may be, we have to expect challenges.

The Wilderness and Valley Experiences

> Then Jesus was led out into the wilderness by the Holy Spirit, to be tempted there by Satan. For forty days and forty nights He ate nothing and became very hungry.
> —Matthew 4:1–2, TLB

Before Jesus could launch His God-given brand, He had to pass a final exam. For forty days and forty nights, Jesus "studied" for His exam through fasting and praying. Christ's studies helped Him to mentally focus, strengthen His will, and fortify His emotions for the various challenges that His God-given brand would have to face as well as its implementation and completion.

I have found that if we choose to follow God at the crossroad of determination, then God will oftentimes lead us into a "study hall" or training session that teaches various principles that will improve upon our abilities to:

1. *Persevere* (Gal. 6:9)—the ability to push through mental, emotional, or physical trauma

2. *Adapt* (Phil. 3:14)—to be mentally and emotionally flexible enough to bend but not break, learn from and adjust to mistakes, obstacles, hindrances, offensive people, make changes for the better

3. *Be fundamentally sound* (Prov. 23:12, Rom. 5:3–4)—adding elements that upgrade our thought processes; give liberty to our emotions within healthy reason; instill the habit of making decisions to do what's right or what's best regardless of what we may want or what someone's opinion, judgment, or rumor may suggest; treat people the way we would like to be treated; be humble and meek

4. *Be wise* (Prov. 4:7–13)—the ability to be strategically sound, manage the soul and its dark side effectively, manage relationships effectively (whether good or bad), manage our brand effectively, show mercy, give grace, teach or train others by either example or by counsel, and be a

tactful and empathetic person: teachable, observant, and vigilantly aware

5. *Be patient* (James 1:4)—the ability to wait for the right moment, avoid hastiness or rash actions, give others time to improve, show mercy, give grace, have compassion, be slow to speak and quick to listen

6. *Be strong* (1 Pet. 5:10)—the ability to tackle tough situations, adversity, overbearing or negative people, temptation and the tactics of the thief; deal with our own shortcomings; admit we are wrong; change; respect others and their choices even if we disagree; fight for what's right or for what's best; possess unwavering faith

7. *Be content* (Heb. 13:5–6)—find peace even when things are hectic or chaotic; be thankful for whatever we have or whoever we're with; to do battle when necessary

Each "study hall" is specifically designed by God to enhance one or more of these seven character traits. For example, the principle of the tree of the knowledge of good and evil was a "study hall" moment for Adam and Eve.

After each "study hall," expect a final exam:

> Then Satan tempted him to get food by changing stones into loaves of bread. "It will prove that you are the son of God," he said.
> —MATTHEW 4:3, TLB

The first problem to be solved in every final exam is overcoming the temptation to use our gifts for self-exaltation, the belittlement of others, or to prey on the disadvantaged.

The structure of this problem will vary according to each individual experience.

In this case, Jesus is dealing with the temptation of self-exaltation (the same temptation Adam and Eve faced).

His gift "to feed" was for the sake of humanity. Christ's fasting and praying was the foundation that made sure that "feeding the souls of men" would be His main focus.

To yield to the temptation to use that gift for personal gratification was out of line, and Christ dealt with it swiftly by using two of the seven character traits:

1. Being strong enough to refuse using His gifts selfishly: *"No! For the scriptures tell us that bread won't feed men's souls..."* (Matt. 4:4a)

2. Being wise enough to humbly continue to follow the plan He and God had put together: *"...obedience to every word of God is what we need"* (Matt. 4:4b)

The next stage in the final exam is found in Matthew 4:5 (TLB):

> Then Satan took him to Jerusalem to the roof of the temple. "Jump off," he said, "and prove you are the Son of God; for the Scriptures declare, 'God will send his angels to keep you from harm,'... they will prevent you from smashing on the rocks below."

The second problem to be solved in every final exam is overcoming "fiery darts" of opposition to your God-given brand's purpose, functionality, and ability to succeed.

Satan's dare is an example of someone poking at another's destiny. He even tried to use the Word of God as an instrument to convince Jesus to do something that He shouldn't. *Note: Please, believers, be mindful not to use the same tactics against each other or against people with different beliefs.*

In this case, the dare was an attempt to refute Christ's identity as the Son of God whose purpose was to save the lost, whose function was to give a better life to all, and whose success would depend upon Christ's confidence in who God had called Him to be.

Christ's response to Satan's dare was simply, *"It also says not to put the Lord your God to a foolish test"* (Matt. 4:7, TLB). His answer incorporates all seven character traits:

1. Though He was physically and maybe even mentally tired, He still had the resiliency to persevere through Satan's badgering of His character and Satan's testing of Christ's will to honor His Father

2. Adapted to Satan's offensive behavior without losing any confidence in His brand or losing any sustenance His brand was capable of providing
   a. Note—when offended, we can sometimes lose a piece of who we are if we allow the offense to alter or damage our character (James 3)

3. Fundamentally able to free His emotions from injury
   a. He knew Satan was up to no good, so He didn't emotionally take offense to Satan's antics

4. Wisely recognizes Satan's request as "foolish"
   a. Jesus understood the true application of His Father's principles
      i. Although Christ *could* have completed the dare, it didn't mean that

He *should*... something we all need to remember when tempted

    ii. If we know that we shouldn't, but we do anyway, then not only are we setting ourselves up for trouble but we are also testing God's grace. *"God will forgive me"* or the submission to the excuse *"nobody's perfect"* is the same frame of mind that got Samson into trouble: *"I will do as before; I'll just shake myself free."* But He didn't know that God had left him (Judg. 16:20), or, *"This time I cannot be blamed for everything I am going to do"* (Judg. 15:3, NLT)

    iii. God will not be mocked. If we get caught up in this behavior, we will reap whatever we sow (Gal. 6:7–8)

5. Able to avoid a rash decision that could have destroyed His destiny

    a. Adam and Eve acted rashly to a similar dare made by Satan about the tree of the knowledge of good and evil, "You won't surely die..." (Gen. 3:4)

        i. Even after their mistake, they failed to take advantage of the "study hall" moment with God by hastily putting the blame on someone else versus taking responsibility for their own actions

6. Christ's faith in the Father and who the Father had predestined Him to be was unwavering

    a. Sometimes these types of circumstances can cause us to question God's intentions: "Why are You letting this happen?"

i. If our faith is unwavering then we will find the strength to deal with the matter even when our emotions have been offended (Job 13:15)
7. Content with having nothing to prove
   a. People dare you in order to prove you're not who you say you are
      i. Knowing who you are gives you the power to overcome such things

The last stage of the final exam is found in Matthew 4:8-9 (TLB):

> Next Satan took him to the peak of a very high mountain and showed him the nations of the world and all their glory. "I'll give it to you," he said, "if you will only kneel and worship me."

This problem is more of a scam than a temptation. You will notice that Satan has taken Jesus somewhere real high for a second time. This tactic is to give the illusion that Satan has more power than he really has. Every thief, hater, naysayer, reformer, or saboteur will use this tactic in the effort to make you or me believe that they have an advantage over us. Here's why:

1. *Your progress causes fear.* Each time you or I deny temptation we inherit character traits that decrease our enemies' ability to form weapons of mass destruction against us (Isa. 54:17).
   a. Therefore, the scam is a defense mechanism to keep you or me from becoming destructive to their plans and purposes.

2. *They're desperate.* You and I have become formidable adversaries.
   a. a. Satan's scam was a result of, "If I can't beat him then I'll invite him to my team."
      i. Beware of people who want to get close to you all of a sudden when they have been so obviously against you.
3. *They're in denial.* Their inability to pull you down into the dungeons of mediocrity, failure, and depression makes them realize that they are in the dungeon alone.
   a. Satan recognizes that his ambition to "be like the most high" has come to an end.
      i. Every tactic he uses today against you or me is an act of desperation. His time is running out and he's trying to ensure that he won't be in the dungeon alone (Rev. 20:7–10, 13–15).
   b. Every hater, naysayer, reformer, or saboteur is miserable in some way, shape, or form, and attacks you and me to ensure that they have someone to keep them company.
      i. Instead of focusing on solutions to their own misery, they focus on causing misery to others.

The scam is also a fear tactic. Sir George Carew's hatred of Dr. Jekyll's kind and giving heart led him to "scare" Dr. Jekyll into feeling inferior and incomplete: *Sir George turns and looks at Dr. Jekyll with malcontent…pauses…and says, "In devoting yourself to others Dr. Jekyll, aren't you neglecting the development of yourself?"*

In Matthew 4:8, Satan took Jesus up high to scare Jesus into quitting His destiny and invites Him to help accomplish his.

Now Jesus's response (Matt. 4:10, TLB) to this problem was very different from the last two. Christ took the humble and meek approach in problems one and two. This time Christ takes a more stern and authoritative approach (pay close attention because this is where many of us fail):

> "Get out of here, Satan," Jesus told him. "The scriptures say, 'Worship only the Lord God. Obey only him.'"

If Christ and Satan were boxers in a ring, then Christ would be Mike Tyson and Satan would be Spongebob Squarepants! Christ busts Satan in the mouth and sends him running:

> Then Satan went away, and angels came and cared for Jesus.
> —MATTHEW 4:11, TLB

Let's take a look at the pugilistic skills Christ used to knock Satan out:

1. The ability to persevere gave Christ stamina. No matter what punch Satan threw at Him, He could take it and give it back.
2. The ability to adapt allowed Christ to bob and weave. Satan was punching but he wasn't hitting anything!
3. The fundamentals of what His Father's principles provided gave Him a strong ring presence. He could be aggressive and push Satan back or frustrate Satan with the "rope-a-dope."

4. Wisdom afforded Him the ability to pick Satan apart. He knew Satan's strategy and could counter at will. Most importantly, He could see Satan's punches even before he threw them (Matt. 26:41; 1 Pet. 5:6).
5. The ability to be patient allowed him to keep Satan at bay with the jab (James 1:4) and position Satan's chin for a right hook, cross, or a vicious uppercut (Isa. 40:31; James 4:7).
6. His strength made Him fearless and determined (Ps. 27:1–6). Satan couldn't intimidate Him (Isa. 26:3–4). Jesus knew He could knock Satan out (Heb. 10:12–13).
7. His contentment with who He was gave Him the energy and the fortitude to fight until the fight was done (2 Tim. 2:3–4).

We can acquire and use these same skills against enemies, our darker selves, and adversities when we make the choice to follow God at the crossroads of determination and learn from each "study hall" moment He provides.

After passing His final exam, Christ was empowered to move forward and launch His God-given brand. He took specific steps:

1. Found the right location and the right time to launch (Matt. 4:12–14)
    a. Where to launch your brand is just as important as when you launch your brand.
        i. Don't be discouraged if your location is small or the timing is not as ideal as you

would like. Sometimes you have to adapt and do what you can with what you have.
  ii. Your launch can consist of anything. What you launch is up to you! It could be a business, a new career, a new relationship, a new perspective, a new look that makes you feel good about yourself, or most importantly (with God's help), the finely tuned and authentic "new" you!
    1. Find your niche and invest in it!
2. Put together a team with different talents and gifts that enhanced the institution and the marketing of His brand
   a. Team had to be teachable (Matt. 4:19)
   b. Team had to respect His authority (Matt. 4:20)
   c. Team had to possess the ability to accomplish assignments and follow instructions (Matt. 10)
   d. Team had to have or be willing to learn good people skills and customer service (Matt. 5:3–16)
   e. Team had to be willing to work together (John 6:1–13)
   f. Team had to be disciplined and receptive to constructive criticism (Luke 9:23–26)
   g. *Every person needs a team; supporters, educators, living examples, and life coaches are important to the stability of your brand personally, socially, or professionally.*
3. Trained His team and provided resources to expand His brand (Matt. 28:18–20; Acts 1:8; chapter 2)

a. Don't be afraid to "train" people
   i. Personally—you train people how to treat you. Know the pros and cons of your own nature and learn how to manage them accordingly. Integrating such skills into your everyday life will produce your ability to respect others and treat them the way they should be treated—or in the case of adversaries, need to be treated.
   ii. Socially—you are who you "say" you are. I'm not talking about lip service; I'm talking about what you do as an individual and for others. Your actions will always speak louder than your words. So practice standing up for who you are and what you believe in, but with tact, with humility, with compassion and empathy, with genuine respect, and always use common sense.
   iii. Professionally—the more resources you provide your team, the more competent, adaptive, and proficient they will become.
b. Doing so could afford you the opportunity to franchise your brand through each "trainee's" individual brand.
   i. They don't become you, but will possess a part of you that will give them an opportunity to launch their own innovative brand. You will get a return on your investment and inspire those you have invested in to invest in someone else.
   ii. As believers we must remember sheep

beget sheep. Goodness begets goodness. The more we become an inspiration to others, the more we can change this world into a better place!
  c. Pay well. I believe if you give your team benefits that make their lives easier, they will have an incentive to work harder and more efficiently for you.
      i. Love those who love you and be kind to those who are kind to you!
      ii. As you grow, feed your team so they can grow too!
      iii. If you own a business, know that you are only as successful as those who work for you!
      iv. Don't be stingy…share the wealth!
          1. Your testimony is powerful and can be a help to someone else.
          2. Pay your employees what they are worth, not what you think they should have.

The question now is, What happens if you fail the final exam? It all depends on the magnitude of your failure. If you are giving a wholehearted effort to follow and learn from God, then by His grace you will be retrained and retested until you get it right. *Note—the higher you go, the more you will be tested up until this life is done.*

The adverse emotions and the collateral damage that come with your failures may not be as bad, or they could be pretty bad but manageable. Even what looks to be unfixable (through God) can be fixed, so hang in there!

Even if you are dealing with an addiction and you relapse, as long as you are giving it your all to escape, then God's grace will continue to empower you to move forward.

But if you half-step, sell yourself short, or are unwilling to change bad behavior that you may have come to love, then be prepared to "fall" into the valley experience:

> "I know you well—you are neither hot nor cold; I wish you were one or the other! But since you are merely lukewarm, I will spit you out of my mouth! You say, 'I am rich, with everything I want; I don't need a thing!' And you don't realize that spiritually you are wretched and miserable and poor and blind and naked.
>
> "My advice to you is to buy pure gold from me, gold purified by fire—only then will you truly be rich. And to purchase from me white garments, clean and pure, so you won't be naked and ashamed; and to get medicine from me to heal your eyes and give you back your sight. I continually discipline and punish everyone I love; so I must punish you unless you turn from your indifference and become enthusiastic about the things of God."
>
> —REVELATION 3:15–19, TLB

Let me make one thing clear. Whether you believe in Jesus Christ or not, you can't expect to go anywhere or become anything by half-steppin'. You're either gonna do what you need to do or you're not. There is no in between. To be in between is to be mediocre or stagnant. Does that sound like greatness to you?

In our text, Jesus is very sternly dispensing tough love. He makes it clear that you can't escape rock bottom or move toward any success with a lukewarm attitude. As a matter of fact, a lukewarm attitude could be the very reason you're at rock bottom.

Or you could be holding on to things or relationships that are weighing you down. Let them go! Your future depends on it!

The valley experience is God's way of giving you and me a reality check. As Jesus states in our text, *"I continually discipline and punish everyone I love; so I must punish you, unless you turn from your indifference..."*

But the valley experience isn't always an "act of God." Nine times out of ten the valley experience is the harvest of what we may have sown. It's the final destination for our irresponsible, hasty, and unwise decisions or behaviors.

But don't be discouraged. In every valley, there is a river of water that gives life and rejuvenation. My river is Jesus Christ:

> If any man thirst, let him come unto me, and drink. He that believeth on me, as the scripture hath said, out of his belly shall flow rivers of living water.
>
> —John 7:37–38

If you fall, get up! Don't stay down; get moving! If you hurt, search for healing that produces a better you! You choose. What do you have to lose? It's all or nothing![1]

As Long As You Get There, Nothing Else Matters

We know how happy they are now because they stayed true to him then, even though they suffered greatly for it. Job is an example of a man who continued to trust the Lord in sorrow; from

> his experiences we can see how the Lord's plan finally ended in good, for he is full of tenderness and mercy.
>
> —JAMES 5:11, TLB

Where are you now? What kind of circumstances are you facing? Can you see the light at the end of the tunnel? If you can see the light, then gear up and run to it!

I know it's hard.

So much darkness surrounds us that it's easy to get lost.

But the light...it's leading you and me to a place that's so much better than where we are.

My wife, my three boys, and I are living at a Motel 6. What about you? Did you lose your home? Car repossessed?

What are you facing now that has dampened your dignity...your self-respect?

Did you lose someone? How bad did it knock you down?

But the light...it feels warm. Warm enough to help us forget what we lost and strive for what is available for us to have.

Yeah, I'm tired too. But if we quit then we'll be stuck where we don't want to be. So we have to continue on.

Who? Oh, don't worry about him. Mr. Hyde is all bark and no bite! He's just a shadow of the real you and me.

The light is our refuge. It's a present help in the time of trouble. Mr. Hyde can't follow us there.

Scared? I was. Now I'm excited. I can see what waits for me in the light. Can't you see yours? It's there.

Our destiny knows our name! It's calling us to come and receive its warm embrace.

That's all right. I doubted at one time or another. But I've learned that God is faithful. His tender mercies can keep us while we're struggling, and His love can fuel our endurance to escape where we are.

As long as we get there, right?

It has been a long and hard-fought journey with many ups and downs.

There may be a few more hills to climb before we make it, but as long as we get there nothing else matters.

Haters? I've had plenty. But that doesn't bother me anymore. My destiny will provide me double for every shame I've had to bear...and yours will too!

Still hurting? I've been there. But I found my healing. I passed my final exam and it gave me the peace I needed. And if I can do it, so can you!

Pain is the agony that is necessary to give birth to our God-given brand.

Congratulations! You are about to give birth to what you can do and what you were born to accomplish!

So stay strong.

Have faith and believe that nothing is impossible! The grandeur of who you are has the power to overcome any obstacle and can make it through the worst of mistakes.

So understand this: When all is said and done, you'll be there...behind the door of enlightenment...standing in the garden of success.

And when you get there, look for me...because I'll be there too!

Your friend,
Steve

NOTES

CHAPTER ONE: CURIOSITY CAN KILL

1. David Wilkerson, *Have You Felt Like Giving Up Lately?* (Grand Rapids, MI: Fleming H. Revell, 2006).
2. David Runcorn, *Choice, Desire, and the Will of God: What more do you want?* (Peabody, MA: Hendrickson Publishers, Inc., 2003), 85–92.
3. *Dr. Jekyll and Mr. Hyde*, film, directed by John S. Robertson (1920: Hollywood, CA: Paramount Pictures).
4. David A. Zimmerman, *Deliver Us From Me-Ville* (Colorado Springs, CO: David C. Cook, 2008), 25–39.

CHAPTER TWO: CONTENTMENT 101

1. Wikipedia.org, s.v. "Invasion of the Body Snatchers," http://en.wikipedia.org/wiki/Invasion_of_the_Body_Snatchers_(1978_film), (accessed December 12, 2010).
2. Runcorrn, *Choice, Desire, and the Will of God*, 93–101.
3. Gene Edward Veith, Jr., *Postmodern Times: A Christian Guide to Contemporary Thought and Culture* (Wheaton, IL: Crossway Books, 1994), 70–90.
4. T.D. Jakes, *Reposition Yourself* (New York: Atria Books, 2007), 1–77.
5. Veith, *Postmodern Times*, 70–90.
6. Noel Jones, *The Battle for the Mind* (Shippensburg, PA: Destiny Image Publishers, 2007), 73–80, 89–94.

CHAPTER THREE: HATERS HATE; THE CHOSEN PERSEVERE

1. Veith, *Postmodern Times*, 70–90.
2. Dr. David Yonggi Cho, *4th Dimensional Living in a 3 Dimensional World.* (Alachua, FL: Bridge-Logos, 2006), 79–116.
3. Benedetto Croce, *Aesthetic as Science of Expression*

and General Linguistic (Lexington, KY: Hardpress Publishing, 2010), 1–24, 49–53.

4. Max Lucado, *He Still Moves Stones* (Nashville, TN: W Publishing Group, 2007), 27–44.

Chapter Four: You Can Run but You Can't Hyde

1. Ray S. Anderson, *The Shape of Practical Theology: Empowering Ministry with Theological Praxis* (Downers Grove, IL: InterVarsity Press, 2001).

2. Runcorn, *Choice, Desire, and the Will of God*, 75–82.

3. Neil Anderson, *The Path to Reconciliation* (Ventura, CA: Regal, 2008). See also James Montgomery Boice, *Romans: The Reign of Grace* (Grand Rapids, MI: Baker Books, 2005); also Jones, *The Battle for the Mind*, 35–41.

Chapter Five: Think About What You're Thinking

1. *Dr. Jekyll and Mr. Hyde*. (Written revisions are based on scenes in the movie.)

2. Cho, *4th Dimensional Living in a 3 Dimensional World*, 29–78. See also Jones, *The Battle for the Mind*, 41–58, 123–144.

3. Bill Johnson, *The Supernatural Power of a Transformed Mind* (Shippensburg, PA: Destiny Image Publishers, 2005).

4. CindyTrimm, *The Rules of Engagement* (Lake Mary, FL: Charisma House, 2008).

5. Henry T. Blackaby and Melvin D. Blackaby, *Experiencing the Resurrection* (Colorado Springs, CO: Multnomah Books, 2008). See also Bill Hybels, *Making Life Work* (Downers Grove, IL: InterVarsity Press, 1998).

Chapter Six: God's Plan, Our Vision

1. Aubrey Malphurs, *Developing a Vision for* Ministry in the 21st Century (Grand Rapids, MI: Baker Books, 2002).

ABOUT THE AUTHOR

Rev. Stephen White has been in the ministry for sixteen years. He accepted his calling into the ministry and was licensed on January 8, 1998 and was ordained on November 27, 1999 by the New Southern Rock Baptist Church under the leadership of Dr. Rudolph White, pastor.

Led by the Holy Spirit, he was self-educated in theology and the Bible. He has preached countless messages at many churches claiming the gospel in the DC, MD, and VA areas. He also has held many positions such as youth minister, minister of music to the youth, men's ministry, young adult, and assistant pastor. Rev. White is supported by his wife Daneisha and three boys; Nehemiah, Joshua, and Caleb.

CONTACT THE AUTHOR

You may contact Rev. Stephen White at
angelmin03@msn.com.